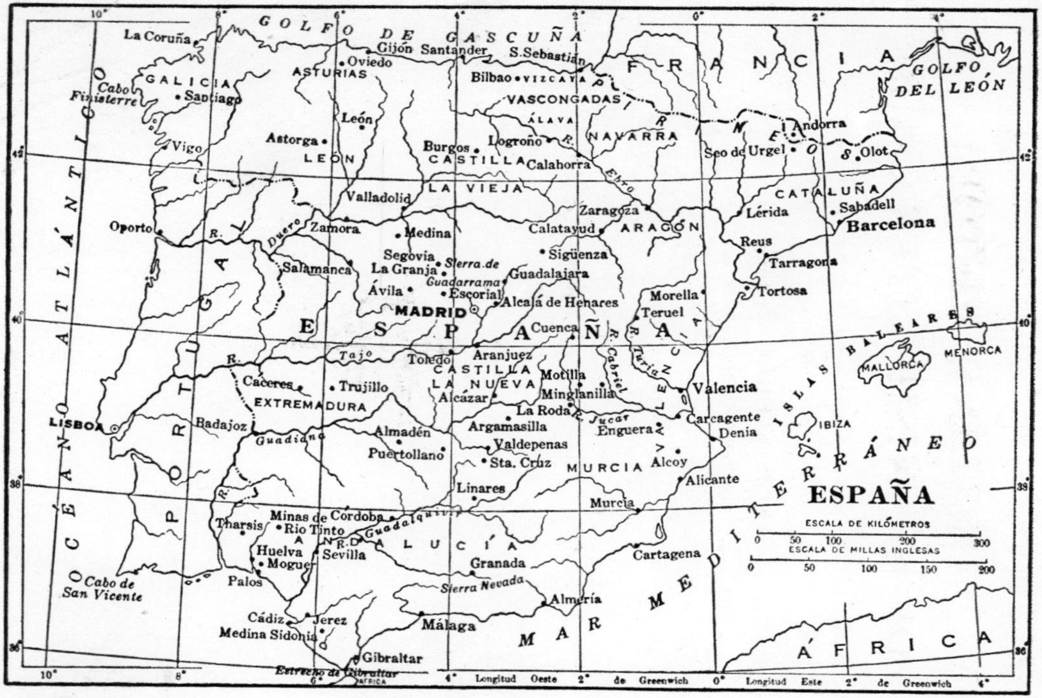
ESPAÑA
ESCALA DE KILÓMETROS
0 50 100 200 300
ESCALA DE MILLAS INGLESAS
0 50 100 150 200
GOLFO DE GASCUÑA
GOLFO DEL LEÓN
FRANCIA
PIRINEOS
OCÉANO ATLÁNTICO
PORTUGAL
ESPAÑA
MAR MEDITERRÁNEO
ISLAS BALEARES
ÁFRICA
GALICIA
ASTURIAS
LEÓN
CASTILLA LA VIEJA
VIZCAYA
VASCONGADAS
ÁLAVA
NAVARRA
ARAGÓN
CATALUÑA
CASTILLA LA NUEVA
EXTREMADURA
VALENCIA
MURCIA
ANDALUCÍA
La Coruña
Cabo Finisterre
Santiago
Vigo
Oporto
LISBOA
Cabo de San Vicente
Oviedo
Gijón
Santander
S. Sebastián
Bilbao
León
Astorga
Burgos
Logroño
Calahorra
Valladolid
Zamora
Medina
Salamanca
Segovia
La Granja
Sierra de Guadarrama
Ávila
Escorial
MADRID
Guadalajara
Alcalá de Henares
Sigüenza
Calatayud
Zaragoza
Andorra
Seo de Urgel
Olot
Lérida
Sabadell
Barcelona
Reus
Tarragona
Tortosa
Morella
Teruel
Cuenca
Aranjuez
Toledo
Tajo
Cáceres
Trujillo
Badajoz
Guadiana
Alcázar
Motilla
Minglanilla
La Roda
Argamasilla
Valdepenas
Sta. Cruz
Almadén
Puertollano
R. Cabriel
R. Turia
R. Jucar
Valencia
Carcagente
Denia
Enguera
Alcoy
Alicante
Murcia
Cartagena
Linares
Minas de Cordoba
Rio Tinto
Tharsis
Huelva
Moguer
Palos
Sevilla
Guadalquivir
Granada
Sierra Nevada
Almería
Málaga
Cádiz
Jerez
Medina Sidonia
Gibraltar
Estrecho de Gibraltar
ÁFRICA
R. Duero
R. Ebro
MALLORCA
MENORCA
IBIZA
Longitud Oeste de Greenwich
Longitud Este de Greenwich
10° 8° 6° 4° 2° 0° 2° 4°
42° 40° 38° 36°

# OUTLINE HISTORY
# OF SPANISH LITERATURE

BY

RALPH STEELE BOGGS, Ph.D.

UNIVERSITY OF NORTH CAROLINA

## D. C. HEATH AND COMPANY

BOSTON

PRINTED IN THE UNITED STATES OF AMERICA

# FOREWORD

THIS outline has been developed through various mimeographed editions over a period of years in the author's own classes. It is based on and indebted to current manuals of Spanish literature and the helpful criticisms of colleagues and students. It is designed for use in the survey course; but advanced students in Spanish, as well as others with a more casual interest, have also found it useful in review and orientation, where a brief and unified picture of Spanish literature or a quick reference is desired. In high schools it will meet the need for a brief study of Spanish literature which is so desirable when the elementary work has been completed.

The divisions of this outline are along the most basic lines of period and type, and may be rearranged easily to suit the wishes of the individual instructor. Corresponding page references to several standard manuals of Spanish literature accompany every section, as a guide to more extensive parallel reading. The chronological table at the end will be found useful for rapid review. For background material and fundamental treatises on various parts of the field, a few further references are given, whenever possible, to works written in English.

For valuable criticism, general suggestions, and correction of details, the author acknowledges his debt of gratitude to Professors S. G. Morley of the University of California, M. A. Buchanan of the University of Toronto, S. N. Treviño of the University of Chicago, E. H. Hespelt of New York University, and S. E. Leavitt of the University of North Carolina.

R. S. B.

UNIVERSITY OF NORTH CAROLINA

iii

# OUTLINE HISTORY OF SPANISH
# LITERATURE

# OUTLINE HISTORY OF SPANISH LITERATURE

## INTRODUCTION

Regionalism is pronounced in Spain, due to variety in physical environment (verdant mountains of Asturias, arid plateaus of Castilla, semitropical gardens of Andalusia), racial mixture (Iberian, Keltic, Roman, Germanic, Arabic), and history (strong Romanization 206 B.C.–409 A.D., Visigothic rulers 409–711, Moslem culture 711–1030). The chief regions of Spain are Galicia, Asturias, the Basque provinces, Navarra, León, Old Castilla, Aragón, Cataluña, Extremadura, New Castilla, Valencia, Andalusia, Granada, and Murcia. Spaniards are highly individualistic, and have a keen sense of personal honor and democracy.

> M. Romera-Navarro: *Historia de la literatura española* (Heath 1928), pp. 3–8; G. T. Northup: *Introduction to Spanish literature* (University of Chicago Press, 2nd ed., 1936), chapter 1; E. Mérimée— S. G. Morley: *History of Spanish literature* (Holt 1930), pp. 3–8; C. E. Chapman: *History of Spain* (Macmillan 1925), chapters 1–6. Hereafter these works will be cited as Rom-Nav., Northup, Mer-Mor., and Chapman, respectively.

## MIDDLE AGE

For 300 years the Spanish Middle Age (mid-12th—mid-15th century) in great part continued the traditions of the entire 1000-year medieval period (5th—mid-15th century).

**I. Beginning of the Spanish language and the character of the Middle Age.**

> Mer-Mor., pp. 17–26, 55–61; Chapman, chs. 7–17.

> A. Latin forms the basis of Spanish; other major elements are Arabic, Greek, French, Italian. Spanish emerged gradually from Vulgar Latin and became an independent

2

language by about the 10th century. Literature was first written in the various dialects, but Castilian early became predominant. Notable linguistic texts of the 10th century are the *Glosas emilianenses* and the *Glosas silenses*.

Rom-Nav., pp. 8–10; Northup, p. 25; Mer-Mor., pp. 8–13.

B. The medieval point of view regarded this life merely as the antechamber to the real life beyond the grave. Prevailing medieval literary traits are morality, didacticism, and allegory. The Catholic Church dominated intellectual activity, although currents of folk traditions have always surged through Spanish literature. There was a general European culture in Latin, and many medieval Spanish literary themes were also current in other countries. There was no idea of plagiarism: writers strove for more modern and more beautiful expression rather than for new material.

II. **Narrative poetry.** Much material of this sort finds expression in the Modern Age in novel form.

A. *Mester de juglaría.* A school of popular poets, all anonymous, using assonating verses of irregular length, averaging sixteen syllables, with a pause in the middle of the verse. This poetic form also is called *mester de juglaría.* It was popular in the 12th and 13th centuries.

1. Folk epic. Flourished in the 12th century. The earlier versions were concerned with patriotic deeds of strength in battle, and were based on Spanish history; in later versions sentimental and fantastic elements became prominent. There are various theories of Spanish epic origin (German, French, Moorish, Latin); possibly the epics were propaganda to attract pilgrims to certain relic centers. Passages in some 13th century historical chronicles, notably the *Crónica general* of Alfonso X (discussed under VI, B, 2), relate the epic themes, and may be prosifications of epics. The erudite epic of the Golden Age (XIII, C) had a short life; but the medieval folk epic themes, known chiefly in history and ballad form, have always been a source of inspiration to Spanish literature.

(a) *Rodrigo el godo.* Preserved only in 13th century prosification. This last Visigothic king seduces a

*In order of events narrated:*

Theories of epic origin:
1. French Origin: Gastón París (Canti-
lena) (1888), Eduardo de Hinojosa
(1904)
2. Germanic Origin: Menéndez Pidal,
Pio Rajnal (1884)
3. Moorish origin: Julián Ribera
4. Propaganda Origin: (written by
monks to attract pilgrims) Joseph Bédier

*La Cava daughter of Count Julián*

girl, loses Spain to the Moors as a result in 711, and
repents. See XXIV, A, 5, *b.*

(*b*) *Roncesvalles* (Battle of, 778). This 100-line *juglaría*
fragment of the early 13th century portrays Carolus
Magnus mourning over his dead heroes on the
battlefield. See XIII, C, 1, *a.*

(*c*) *Bernardo del Carpio.* Preserved only in 13th century
prosification. He is the only non-Castilian (Leonese)
and only fictitious epic hero. He supposedly lived
in the late 8th century. Child of an unhappy love,
he discovers his identity, and finally wins the freedom
of his father, — cold in death. See XIII, C, 1, *a* and
XIV, A and XXV, B, 3, *b.*

(*d*) *Fernán González.* Preserved in a *clerecía* poem
(II, B, 2, *a*). This late 10th century count of Castilla
wins independence from León by the sale of a horse
and a hawk. Freed from prison by a princess in
Navarra, he rewards her by marrying her.

(*e*) *Siete infantes de Lara* or *Salas.* Preserved only in
13th century prosification. It is the story of a late
10th century feud; the infantes' death is avenged by
their half brother, Mudarra. See XIV, A and
XXIV, A, 2, *b* and XXV, B, 3, *a.*

(*f*) *Cerco de Zamora.* Preserved only in 13th century
prosification. An ambitious late 11th century king
tries to reunite a kingdom and is treacherously
murdered. This poem shows a spirit of compromise
between Castilla and León, and is the most truly
national of all.

(*g*) *Poema de Mío Cid.* A *juglaría* poem, composed
about 1140, first printed in 1779 (XXIII, B). The
Cid is banished, he wins Valencia from the Moors, is
reconciled with the king, who makes an unfortunate
marriage for the Cid's daughters. The tradition of
the Cid (died 1099) represents the height of epic development. See XXIII, B, 2, *d* and XXIX, D.

*Story first referred to in Crónica de 1344*

(*h*) *Rodrigo, Crónica rimada,* or *Mocedades del Cid.* A
*juglaría* poem, written about 1400. It tells of the
Cid's youthful exploits and his marriage to Jimena.
This story, rather than the *Poema de Mío Cid,* is the
basis of later literary exploitation of the Cid story.
See XIV, E.

(*i*) *Poema de Alfonso XI.* In quatrains of eight-syllable

Summary of ~~method~~ form of preservation
-------- -- ------- -- -----------

Preserved in mester de juglaría :
   1) Poema de mío Cid (ca. 1140)
   2) Roncesvalles fragment (13th c.)
   3) Rodrigo (Crónica Rimada ) (ca. 1400)

Preserved in prosificaciones :
   1) Rodrigo el godo (13th c.)
   2) Bernardo del Carpio (13th c.)
   3) Siete Infantes de Lara (13th c.)
   4) Cerco de Zamora (13th c.)

Preserved in mester de clerecía :
   1) Fernán González (between 1250 + 1271 ?)

Preserved in other form :
   1) Poema de Alfonso XI (mid 14th c.)
     octosyllabic quatrains, riming ABAB

verses rimed ABAB, composed about the mid-14th century. It tells of this powerful king's (ruled 1312–1350) struggles against the Moors. This poem seems to be a link between epic and ballad.

Rom-Nav., pp. 13–21, 43; Northup, ch. 2 and p. 65; Mer-Mor., pp. 26–37, 86–87.

2. Other *juglaría* poems. Chiefly disputes and pious biographies of the 13th century, mostly in rimed couplets, with some assonance and irregularity of rime, of varying verse lengths, often approaching ballad meter. The themes treated were generally current in European literature.

(a) *Disputa del alma y el cuerpo.* In a 37-line fragment the soul rebukes the body for its wicked life.

(b) *Razón de amor; con los denuestos del agua y el vino.* Two distinct works written together: the first real Castilian love lyric, and a debate of drys against wets.

*last ç 13ᵗʰ C* (c) *Elena y María.* In a strongly satiric vein two girls dispute on the merits of their lovers: knight against cleric.

*in same MS*

(d) *Santa María Egipciaca.* Relates the adventures and penance of Egypt's gayest streetwalker.

(e) *Libro de los tres reyes de Oriente.* Tells of the adoration of Jesus and the flight into Egypt.

Rom-Nav., p. 28; Northup, pp. 57–59; Mer-Mor., pp. 47–50.

B. *Mester de clerecía.* A school of erudite poets, using monorimed quatrains of regular fourteen-syllable verses, with a pause in the middle of the verse. This poetic form is called *cuaderna vía.* It was popular in the 13th and 14th centuries.

1. Clerical themes: saints' lives and Church history.

*(1180 ?– 1246 ?)* (a) Gonzalo de Berceo (early 13th century). This priest of Old Castilla, the earliest known author in Spanish literature, popularized in Spanish edifying Latin works, in a simple style, with rustic humor, lofty inspiration, and a rich vocabulary. He wrote about 13,000 lines: three saints' lives (*Vida de santo Domingo de Silos* is the best), three poems on the Virgin (*Milagros de Nuestra Señora* is the best, including several famous exempla — see V, A), three other

*Sources: Gautier de Coincy, Les miracles de la Sainte Vierge*

— early 13ᵗʰ c.

— 8/7/9 syll. lines, rhymed couplets

} 9/8 syllable lines

Libro de Alexandre (13ᵗʰ c.) : " mester trago
fermoso, no es de joglaría; | mester es sin
puccado, ca es de clerezia : | fablar curso
rimado por la quaderna vía, | a síllavas
cuntadas, ca es grant maestría."

{ Vida de Santo Domingo de Silos
  Vida de San Millán de la Cogolla
  Vida de Santa Aurea u Oria, Virgen

{ Milagros de Nuestra Señora
  Loores de Nuestra Señora
  Duelos que fizo la Virgen el día de la
      Pasión

religious poems (*De los signos que aparecerán ante del juicio*, of the terrible prodigies to appear before Judgment Day, is the best), and three hymns.

(*b*) *Poema de Yuçuf* or *José*. This early 14th century anonymous poem is based on the Koran and rabbinical writings, and tells of the Biblical Joseph and Potiphar's wife (see V, A, 3). It is the best example of *aljamiada* literature (Spanish written in Arabic characters).

Rom-Nav., pp. 8, 22–26; Northup, pp. 59–61, 64–65; Mer-Mor., pp. 38–42, 46–47.

2. Secular themes: of worldly heroes and social satire.

(*a*) 13th century anonymous poems. *Libro de Apolonio* is a romance of shipwrecks and reunions, the first Milesian tale in Spanish (see XV, E), probably from a Greek original. *Libro de Alejandro* is about Alexander the Great (356–323 B.C.) as the perfect medieval knight, his deeds and marvelous yarns of the Orient; an encyclopedic display of erudition in a brilliant style. *Poema de Fernán González* (see II, A, 1, *d*) is the only *clerecía* poem of an epic theme.

(*b*) Juan Ruiz, Archpriest of Hita (1283?–1350?). His *Libro de buen amor* (written around the 1330's) is the autobiography of a rascal who knew the game of love. He says we should strive for *buen amor* (spiritual love), but he gives a colorful and intriguing portrayal of worldly love, with much keen satire. This work is of miscellaneous content, including excellent lyrics (*serranillas;* religious songs to the Virgin, and blind beggars' songs). His Trotaconventos, an old woman go-between, is Celestina's (XI, B) prototype. In a personal, vigorous style, he gives a vivid picture of the lower classes. The episode of *Don Melón y doña Endrina* is dramatic in its dialogue. This work is the best of the *clerecía* type.

(*c*) Pedro López de Ayala (1332–1407). His *Rimado de palacio* (written about 1400) is the autobiography of a statesman and courtly gentleman who, with moral gravity and bitter satire, vividly portrays court life. He also includes some fine lyrics in *arte*

El martirio de San Lorenzo
Sacrificio de la misa
De los signos que aparecerán antes del juicio
Hymns: "Veni Creator," Ave Maris Stella," "Christus
qui lux "
(Paraphrased translations of Latin)


2600 some verses

more than 10,000 verses

*mayor* (see II, C), and miscellaneous material.  See
VI, B, 3 for his historical works.  His *Rimado* is the
last great work in *cuaderna vía.*

Rom-Nav., pp. 18, 22–23, 26–27, 47–48, 50–55;  Northup,
pp. 34, 61–64, 101–110;  Mer-Mor., pp. 42–46, 76–84.

C. *Danza de la Muerte* (early 15th century).  This anonymous
poem is written in *arte mayor*, eight-line stanzas, rimed
typically ABABBCCB, with a verse structure based on
accents rather than syllables: four accents to each verse,
with a pause in the middle of the verse — two accents
to each half line.  Death levels all: Pope and emperor,
painted ladies and rascally lawyers, — all must dance to
Death's grim tune.  This poem is keen in satire and super-
ficially dramatic in form.  The theme was very popular
in medieval literature and art.  The Spanish version is the
finest preserved.  See X, C, 1.

*12 syllables?*

Northup, pp. 66–67;  Mer-Mor., pp. 87–88.

## III. Lyric poetry.

[A. GALICIAN-PORTUGUESE.  Flourished in the 12th–14th centuries.  Native genius and Provençal models were fused to
express love and satire in artificial forms.  The Galician
dialect was used by cultured Spanish lyric poets almost
exclusively until the 14th century.  Over 2000 poems by
some 200 known poets are preserved of this courtly school.
Alfonso X's (VI, A) *Cántigas de Santa María* (late 13th
century) comprise more than 400 poems, mostly miracles
of the Virgin.  Other important collections are: *Cancioneiro
da Ajuda, Cancioneiro portuguez da Vaticana, Canzoniere
portoghese Colocci-Brancuti.*

Rom-Nav., pp. 28–32;  Northup, pp. 98–101;  Mer-Mor.,
pp. 51–54, 65–66.]

B. EARLY CASTILIAN.  Flourished in the 13th–14th centuries.
Little is preserved, probably due to the popularity of
Galician-Portuguese poetry and to oral circulation of Cas-
tilian lyrics.  Possibly this poetry is based somewhat on
Arabic models of Andalusia (J. Ribera's theory)  First
traces of Castilian lyrics are found in Berceo's (II, B, 1, *a*)
*Duelo de la Virgen* (the watchman's song), *Razón de amor*

C. da Ajuda ( ca. 1300
                early 14th c. )
       302 poems - 38 poets
C. da Vaticana ( ca. 1500)
       1205 songs

C. da Biblioteca Nacional (Colocci - Brancuti)
       1647 songs

(II, A, 2, *b*), *Libro de buen amor* (II, B, 2, *b*), *Rimado de palacio* (II, B, 2, *c*).

Rom-Nav., pp. 27–28;  Northup, pp. 97–98;  Mer-Mor., p. 54.

C.  COURTLY.  Flourished chiefly in the time of Juan II (ruled 1406–1454), a great patron of literature.  Great collections of this poetry are: *Cancioneros* of Baena (1445?–1454?), Stúñiga (1460?), Hernando del Castillo (1511), García de Resende (1516).  They include much allegoric and love poetry, of superficial elegance, lacking roots in the soil, *muchas poesías, poca poesía* (much in quantity, little in quality), with troubador and Italian and Classic influences. Humanistic traits (VII, B) begin to appear (Santillana and Mena).  The popular poetic form in the 15th century was the *arte mayor* (see II, C).

*[handwritten margin note: mainly Portuguese]*

1.  Íñigo López de Mendoza, Marquis of Santillana (1398–1458).  This cultured statesman's prose *Proemio y carta al Condestable de Portugal* (1449) is the first important critical work on Spanish poetry.  In it he stresses form, condemns popular *romances y cantares* (yet his own inspiration is often from the folk), supports artistic poetry and Classic rules, and is influenced chiefly by the Italian and Galician poets.  Santillana is the most important poet of this group.

(*a*) Troubador and popular poetry (*canciones, decires, serranillas*).  Express delicate sentiment with a natural elegance of form.

(*b*) Allegoric poetry.  Shows Italian influence, of Dante (1265–1321) and Petrarch (1304–1374).  Dramatic in form, but really a poem in *arte mayor*, is the *Comedieta de Ponza* (1444), on the defeat of the kings of Aragón and Navarra in a naval battle against Genoa in 1435 near the Isle of Ponza.

*[handwritten margin note: 12 syllables ABABBccB]*

(*c*) Sonnets.  In fourteen eleven-syllable verses, rimed typically ABAB, ABAB, CDC, DCD, Santillana's 42 sonnets are said to be the first ever written in Spanish.

2.  Juan de Mena (1411–1456).  This Andalusian, and Latin secretary to Juan II, resided in Italy, and was influenced chiefly by Italian and Classic models.  He

Cancionero de Baena : 576 poems by 54 poets + 35 anon. works : Older Gal. - Port. type poets represented by Alfonso Álvarez de Villasandino (1350 - 1428?) - & Macías. Later groups headed by Micer Francisco Imperial, Genoese in Seville, introduced _ hendecasyllable into Spain.

did much to popularize the *arte mayor*. He enriched the
language and developed a special poetic vocabulary.
His best work is *Las trescientas* or *El laberinto de For-
tuna* (1444?), an allegory inspired by Dante's *Paradiso*
(1300?). The author visits various social or moral
groups in seven circles on each of Fortune's three wheels.

3. Jorge Manrique (1440?–1479). This soldier poet was
made famous by a single poem: *Coplas a la muerte de su
padre* (in 1476), which sings the theme of Death and the
futility of human striving, and merges personal with
universal emotion. It is written in twelve-line stanzas
alternating two lines of eight syllables with one line of
four syllables, riming ABcABcDEfDEf. Longfellow's
first literary work was an excellent English translation of
this poem in 1833.

4. *Coplas de Mingo Revulgo* (late 15th century). This
anonymous pastoral allegory in dialogue is a political
satire in popular tone, contrasting with other courtly
poetry. (Other popular anonymous political satiric
*coplas* in the 15th century are: *Coplas de ¡ Ay panadera !*
and *Coplas del Provincial.*)

*[margin handwritten note: attacks King Henry IV (1454–74)]*

> Rom-Nav., pp. 60–75; Northup, pp. 110–119; Mer-Mor.,
> pp. 101–114, 122–129.

**IV. Drama.** *Juglares* and popular entertainers probably fur-
nished the folk with drama. Religious drama grew out of
Church liturgy and celebrations of themes from the Christmas,
Epiphany, and Easter cycles, Bible stories, saints' lives, and
allegoric moralities. Plays were performed on holidays and at
courtly festivals. A law in the *Siete partidas* (VI, A), regulating
drama, proves there were religious and profane dramas, spoken,
performed inside and outside the Church, acted by clerics and
laity, for money, and often the clergy was ridiculed in *juegos
de escarnio*. Popular dramatists probably wrote in eight-
syllable ballad verse, erudite dramatists in *arte mayor*.

*Auto* or *Misterio de los Reyes Magos* (mid-12th century).
The Wise Men decide to test the Christ Child to see if he is
the promised king, tell Herod of His birth, and depart;
Herod consults his astrologers. Here the fragment breaks
off after some 150 lines of varied metrical structure: six,
eight, and twelve-syllable rimed verses. This version is
primitive in character, probably after a Latin model;

Coplas del Provincial (149 coplas) (1465-1474?)
   satire against ladies of court
Coplas de ¡ Ay panadera! satire on
   cowardice in battle of Olmedo in 1445

simple, dignified, and clerical in style. It is the only good
example preserved of a medieval Spanish drama, and is one
of the finest examples of plays on this theme in medieval
Europe.

> Rom-Nav., p. 108; Northup, pp. 53–57; Mer-Mor., pp.
> 50–51; J. P. W. Crawford: *Spanish drama before Lope de
> Vega* (Philadelphia 1922), ch. 1.

**V. Novelistic prose.**    Short tales and longer prose works of
miscellaneous content and novelistic character are medieval
predecessors of the modern novel.

A. Exempla.   Short stories with a moral point, written in the
13th–15th centuries, mingling Oriental morals (material-
istic) of self-preservation with Christian morals (idealistic)
of sacrifice and brotherly love. These are usually large
anonymous collections with a framework. The typical
line of transmission of Oriental material is from Sanskrit
(in ancient India) to Persian, to Arabic, to Latin or Spanish,
thence to the rest of Europe. However, much native
European material was added. See II, B, 1, *a*.

[1. *Disciplina clericalis* (early 12th century). Written in
Latin by Petrus Alfonsi, a converted Aragonese Jew.
It contains thirty excellent stories in a frame, and was
widely incorporated into later collections.]

2. *Calila y Dimna* (1251). This anonymous translation
from Arabic, by order of Alfonso the Wise (VI, A), is
based in good part on that Sanskrit masterpiece, the
*Panchatantra*. It contains many animal tales, often
satirizing social classes. The philosophic discussions
of Calila and Dimna, two lynxes, constitute the chief
frame. This is the oldest Spanish fictional prose.

3. *Libro de los engaños y asayamientos de las mujeres* (1253).
This famous anonymous Spanish version of the *Dolo-
pathos*, *Syntipas*, *Sindibad*, or *Seven wise masters* material was translated from Arabic by order of Fadrique,
Alfonso X's brother. Licentious stories illustrate the
deceits and wiles of women. Compare the story of
Joseph and Potiphar's wife (see II, B, 1, *b*). A youth
falsely accused of attempted seduction by his young
stepmother (whereas she really tried to seduce him)
constitutes the frame. This work and the *Corbacho*

Tr. from Sanskrit to Pehlevi by Barzuyeh on order of Cosroes I, king of Persia (531-70)

(V, C, 2) are the best medieval examples expressing
scorn of woman (the contrary of XI, C).

4. *Barlaam y Josaphat* (13th century). This anonymous
collection goes back to the *Lalita Vistara*, of Buddha's
(Josaphat) youth.  He is reared in perfect sensual
happiness, but finally encounters old age, sickness,
poverty, and death.  Barlaam, his tutor, explains these,
and Josaphat turns to religion.  This frame gives oppor-
tunity for many illustrative exempla.

5. Juan Manuel (1282–1348).  This prince's best work is
his *Conde Lucanor* or *Libro de Patronio* (1330–1335.)
Written many years before Boccaccio's *Decameron*
(1348–1353), these stories, in a slight frame of a prince
seeking advice from his tutor, are taken from a variety
of well-chosen sources, and told in a pleasant manner.
Juan Manuel contributed much to the development of
Spanish prose; his language is rich, his expression clear
and simple, and his style personal.  He wrote several
didactic works, including a *Crónica abreviada* (after 1337)
which is a summary of the *Crónica general* (VI, B, 2) of
his uncle Alfonso X, and a *Libro del caballero y del
escudero* (1326) suggested by a similar work of the
Catalan, Raymond Lull (1235–1315), on the perfect
knight.   *(1370?–1426)   before 1434)*

6. Clemente Sánchez de Vercial (early 15th century).
Compiled the *Libro de los ejemplos por abc*, arranged
alphabetically by the first word in a Latin couplet at
the head of each tale, expressing the moral illustrated,
for convenient use by preachers.  This is the largest
(nearly 500) *520* of the exempla collections.

Rom-Nav., pp. 33, 37, 44–46; Northup, pp. 79–87; Mer-
Mor., pp. 66–70, 72–74.

B. CHIVALRIC ROMANCES.  Mostly 14th century anonymous
prose adventures of sentimental knightly heroes, replacing
the earlier epics of strong, two-fisted warriors.  Magic and
love elements are important, and much material came
from French sources.  This type did not reach its full
flower until the Renascence (see XI, A).

1. Material of king Arthur, his knights, and the Holy
Grail.

2. Material of Carolus Magnus and his peers.

Juan García de Castrojeriz compiled Castigos
y Documentos in mid 14th c. Similar to
Disciplina clericalis, partly adapted from
Egidio Colonna's De regimine principum

Libro de los gatos (14th c.) based on
Narrationes of English Odo of Cheriton
6 7 tales                                    (+1247)

Cf. William J. Entwistle, The Arthurian
Legend in the Literatures of the Spanish
Peninsula (London, 1925)
        Anales toledanos primeros (1215) have
first mention of Arthur in Castile.

3. Material of antiquity. *Historia troyana* (about 1270) treats the story of Troy, in prose and verse.

4. Material of the Crusades. *La gran conquista de ultramar* (early 14th century) is a long and fabulous account of the Crusades up to 1271, and brings to Spanish literature many chivalric themes, especially the story of Lohengrin, the swan knight.

*Pub. 1512* 5. *El caballero Cifar* (written about 1300). Varied content: *Not (1&2)*a Milesian tale (see XV, E for definition of this type), *popular (3)*exempla, proverbs. This is the oldest original Spanish chivalric romance.

6. *Amadis de Gaula.* Evidently this story circulated in the 14th century, but we know it only in Montalvo's reworking of 1508 (XI, A, 1).

Rom-Nav., pp. 37–39, 97–100; Northup, pp. 88–93; Mer-Mor., pp. 70–72, 75–76, 135–140.

C. OTHER NOVELISTIC PROSE.

1. *Purgatorio de san Patricio* (13th century). An anonymous adaptation of H[enry] of Saltrey's Latin account (late 12th century) of St. Patrick's experiences in a cave in Ireland, in which the joys of Heaven and horrors of Hell are revealed to him. The bulk of the work tells of Owein's later visit there. Lope de Vega, Calderón, and others have dramatized this theme.

2. Alfonso Martínez de Toledo, Archpriest of Talavera (1398–1470 ?). His *Corbacho* or *Reprobación del amor mundano* (1438), like the Italian Boccaccio's *Corbaccio* (1355), is a bitter satire against the vices of women: *wrote also* flirt, adulteress, gossip, conceited beauty, — all are *Atalaya de* "whipped" by his keen words (see V, A, 3). He knew *las crónicas* his subject well, and gives a good insight into the private and everyday life of women of his day. This work contributed greatly to flowing, popular, conversational prose, and is an important source of the *Celestina* (XI, B).

Rom-Nav., pp. 92–96; Northup, pp. 87–88; Mer-Mor., pp. 118–120.

**VI. Didactic literature.** *born 1221*

A. ALFONSO X, el Sabio (ruled 1252–1284). This greatest medieval patron of letters was a pioneer developer of

Divided into 4 parts: (1) El cavallero de Dios (2) El Rey de Mentón (3) Castigos del Rey de Mentón (= Çifar )( to his sons), (4) Los hechos de Roboán (son of Çifar) ⊕ most like novel of chivalry.

Mention as being in 3 books by Gal-Port. poet Pedro Ferrús (†1379), represented in Cancionero de Baena (1445)

Parts of Corbacho: I. Sins caused by women. II. Evil qualities of women. III. Different characters produced by humours: sanguine, choleric, phlegmatic, melancholic, + relation with signs of Zodiac. IV. Fates, fortunes + signs + how they are controlled by God.

Spanish prose: he directed and financed encyclopedic
compilations in Spanish from great Arabic, Hebrew, and
Latin works of literature and science, which spread from
his court to the rest of Europe. His *Siete partidas* (begun
about 1256) is one of the world's greatest codifications of
laws. He produced works on astronomy (about 1277),
a *Lapidario* (finished 1279) which describes precious stones
and their magic qualities, works on games such as chess and
dice (finished 1283), great historical works (VI, B, 2), and
lyric poetry (III, A).

> Rom-Nav., pp. 33–35; Northup, pp. 69–73; Mer-Mor., pp.
> 61–63, 64–65.

B. History.

[1. The early 13th century Latin histories of Lucas of Tuy
and Rodrigo of Toledo were important sources for
Alfonso X.]

2. Alfonso X's histories. His *Crónica general* (begun about
1264) of Spain is the most important history written
in the Middle Age. It accepts legend as well as fact
(see II, A, 1). It is a fine attempt to fix Spanish prose
usage. It was reworked in the *Crónica general de 1344;*
a still later version, the *Tercera crónica general*, published
by Ocampo (XII, A, 1, c) in 1541, was the only version
in print until 1906. Alfonso's *Grande y general historia* (begun about 1265) of the world is a vast compila-
tion from Biblical and varied sources.

3. Pedro López de Ayala's (see II, B, 2, c) chronicles. Of
*[handwritten: Imitated Livy ab urbe condita]* Pedro el Cruel (ruled 1350–1369), Enrique II (ruled
1369–1379), Juan I (ruled 1379–1390), Enrique III
(ruled 1390–1406) furnish a vivid history of the author's
own period, and bring a new personal note to history
writing, with fine character analyses in excellent prose.

4. Fernán Pérez de Guzmán (1376?–1460?). His *Mar de
[handwritten: nephew of Ayala]* *historias* (written in the 1440's) is a collection of biographies. Best is the third part, *Generaciones y sem-
blanzas*, which vividly characterizes his contemporaries.

*[handwritten: See p. 44]*

> Rom-Nav., pp. 35–37, 46–47, 83–88; Northup, pp. 73–79;
> Mer-Mor., pp. 63–64, 71, 82–83, 114–116.

C. Proverbs. In the Middle Age proverbs (maxims rather
than real folk proverbs) were regarded as the essence of

Alfonso's works in chronological order:

1. Las tablas alfonsíes (1252)
2. Los libros de astronomía (ca. 1256-77)
3. El septenario (1256-63)
4. Las siete partidas (1256-65)
5. Las cantigas (1257-75)
6. Primera crónica general (1264 - reign of Sancho IV)
7. La grande e general Istoria (1265-80)
8. El lapidario (1276-79)
9. Libros de ajedrez, dados y tablas (finished 1283)

(d. 1249)
El Tudense, Chronicon mundi

Rodrigo de Toledo (d. 1247) - Historia gothica

(also called: De rebus Hispaniae

human knowledge and experience. They abound throughout Spanish literature. Typical 13th century examples are:
*Bocados de oro* and *Libro de los buenos proverbios;* 14th
century: *Proverbios morales* of the rabbi Sem Tob; 15th
century: the marquis of Santillana's (authorship not
established) *Refranes que dicen las viejas tras el fuego.* The
first three collections are rather erudite; the last is rather
popular.

*1358 To 1369*

Rom-Nav., pp. 33, 44, 67; Northup, pp. 65–66; Mer-Mor.,
pp. 74–75, 84–86, 107–108.

# MODERN AGE

The Modern Age (mid-15th century—present day) was ushered
in by the revolutionary period of the Renascence (mid-15th—mid-
16th century), which broke definitively with medieval traditions,
and by ennobling native genius with Italian-interpreted Classicism,
flowered in the Golden Age (mid-16th—mid-17th century), which
declined rapidly (late 17th century); reacted with Neoclassicism
(18th century); returned to native traditions and regionalism
(19th century); and now seeks a broader nationalism (20th century). Underlying the fluctuations of these last five centuries, the
new traditions of the Modern Age, established by the Renascence,
have endured. The bedrock of native Spanish traditions has always
survived all changes, both medieval and modern.

# RENASCENCE

## VII. Renascence and Humanism.

A. Renascence means "rebirth" of interest in this life and in
   man.

   1. General European traits: origins in Italy; Humanism
      — shifting center of interest from spiritual to human
      life; art for art's sake; spirit of criticism and experi-
      mentation; voyages of exploration; development of
      printing; of individualism and will power; of realism
      and sensualism; of interest in the Classics; revival of
      Platonism (a cult of idealized love); the Reformation;
      secularization of education.

2. Special Spanish traits: many Renascence traits were already typically Spanish (individualism, realism, regional culture); old traditions continued along with acceptance of the new, hence there was no sharp break with the Middle Age; *Les trobes en lahors de la Verge Marie* (Valencia 1474) is the first printed book known in Spain. Strong unity and peace prevailed in Spain, safeguarded by the Inquisition from bloody religious wars as seen in northern Europe: political unity under Fernando and Isabel (ruled jointly 1474–1504); religious and territorial unity with expulsion of Jews and Moors (1492); linguistic unity, as Castilian predominated as the literary language. Carlos V (ruled 1516–1556) governed one of the greatest empires in world history. Spain established her culture in the New World.

Rom-Nav., pp. 59–60, 123–130; Northup, pp. 122–130; Mer-Mor., pp. 93–100; Chapman, chs. 18–22.

B. SPANISH HUMANISTS. Followed Italy in studying, translating, and imitating the Classics. Increasing interest in Humanism is seen early in the 15th century (III, C, 1 and 2). Interest in Hebrew and Biblical studies is particularly Spanish.

1. Elío Antonio de Lebrija or Nebrija (144 ?–1522). From Andalusia, he resided awhile in Italy. [He wrote a Latin grammar in 1481.] His Spanish grammar (1492) is the first scientific grammar of any modern language. He also produced a Latin-Spanish vocabulary (1492). He did much to fix Castilian spelling and usage.

2. Cardinal Jiménez de Cisneros (1436–1517). Founded the great Renascence University of Alcalá de Henares (1508), and sponsored the Polyglot Bible (1514–1517), with Hebrew, Caldaic, Greek, and Latin texts, the result of collaboration of great scholars (including Nebrija), and the first critical edition of the Bible.

3. Juan de Valdés (died 1541) and his brother Alfonso (died 1532). Alfonso's *Diálogo de Mercurio y Carón* (1528) shows Protestant sympathies. Juan led an unorthodox religious group in Naples in the 1530's. His *Diálogo de la lengua* (about 1535) includes comments on literary works and nearly 200 proverbs, and is one of the most brilliant linguistic treatises ever written. His

religious doctrines are expressed in *Ciento y diez consi-
deraciones divinas* (1539). He is a master of dialogue
and one of the best stylists and prose writers of the 16th
century.

4. Antonio de Guevara (1480?–1545). His *Reloj de prin-
   cipes con el libro de Marco Aurelio* (1529) is a didactic
   novel, long popular through Europe, on the perfect
   prince. His *Década de Césares* (1539) gives biographies
   of ten Roman emperors. Guevara was a painstaking
   stylist.

Rom-Nav., pp. 60, 124, 168–172; Northup, pp. 130–134,
225–228; Mer-Mor., pp. 100, 154–156, 185–191, 192–195.

**VIII. Lyric poetry.** The struggle between, and mingling of
Italian and native forms characterizes this period.

A. ITALIANATE. Imitated Italian and Classic verse forms,
   gained formal perfection, and sought fantastic material
   of the imagination (mythology and pastoral scenes).

*Pub. 1534*

*Persuaded to try It. meters by Andrea Navagiero, Venetian ambassador in Spain*

1. Juan Boscán Almogaver (1493?–1542). This Catalan
   translated Castiglione's *Courtier* (1528), the Italian
   Renascence manual of the modern gentleman, into
   excellent Spanish prose in 1533. He wrote between
   thirty and forty native *coplas* (usually ten eight-syllable lines to a stanza, the first five lines with some AB
   rime pattern, the last five with CD). His widow published his collected verse, along with that of Garcilaso
   de la Vega, in 1543. Boscán was the first to naturalize
   Italian verse forms in Castilian (beginning 1527), especially eleven-syllable verse, popular with Spanish poets
   ever since. The royal octave (stanzas of eight eleven-
   syllable lines, rimed ABABABCC), which was the meter
   of the Italian erudite epic masters, Ariosto (1474–1533)
   and Tasso (1544–1595), became the Spanish erudite epic
   meter (XIII, C). Boscán wrote 92 sonnets. For the
   eleven-syllable verse and sonnet see III, C, 1, *c*. He is
   more important as the initiator of a movement than as a
   poetic genius.

2. Garcilaso de la Vega (1501?–1536). Was a living model
   of the Renascence gentleman. He resided awhile in
   Italy, was active in war and politics, and led a fast and
   furious life. He wrote a small quantity of polished,
   *Died attacking a tower of M mey in Provence.*

Luis Vives (1492-1540)

1520-1557. Gutierre de Cetina, 5
madrigals including "Ojos claros,
serenos"

*addressed to Boscán* →

musical verse: 38 sonnets, 5 *canciones*, 3 eclogues, 2 elegies, an *epístola;* also 8 native *coplas*, written in his youth. Love and nature were his chief inspirations. He is the best Renascence master of form, perfect finish, simplicity, and fluidity attained by careful workmanship. This poetic genius made the eleven-syllable verse elegant and graceful.

Rom-Nav., pp. 131–139; Northup, pp. 136–139; Mer-Mor., pp. 160–167.

B. TRADITIONAL. Was well sustained despite the Italianate poetry.

Cristóbal de Castillejo (1490?–1550). *Contra los que dejan los metros castellanos y siguen los italianos* (probably written in the 1540's) is typical of his polemic verse. His collected works were not published until 1573. His poetry is satiric, of varied inspiration, chiefly erotic and religious, and often colorful in content. He was the champion traditionalist

Rom-Nav., pp. 139–143; Northup, pp. 139–140; Mer-Mor., pp. 167–170.

IX. **Ballad.** This epico-lyric and most typical of Spanish verse forms has an average eight-syllable line, with the last stress on the seventh syllable (half a sixteen-syllable line?); with odd lines blank, even lines assonating, and no stanzaic grouping (later developments produced various rime schemes and quatrain groupings); is dramatic and fragmentary in style, portraying high points in a hero's life. There are five types: (1) *romances históricos*, national, historical fragments, dealing with heroes of the 12th and 13th century epics; (2) *juglarescos*, romantic, marvelous 14th century epic material, often not national (see II, A, 1 and V, B); (3) *fronterizos*, or border ballads, of struggles between Christians and Moors in the 15th century, vivid scenes of intimate incidents, often historic, and apparently by an eyewitness; (4) *eruditos*, by known, cultured poets, imitating ballad style, based on material found in chronicles, especially Ocampo's edition (XII, A, 1, *c*) of Alfonso X's *Crónica general* in 1541; (5) *artísticos*, by contemporary poets, in ballad style, made predominantly lyric, on any theme (pastoral, *morisco*, religious, roguish); also occasional and vulgar forms. See XIII, B. Ballads are transmitted

← Bucolic influences : Virgil + Sannazaro
  amorous influences
  1 Luis de León (1527-91), p. 48

  1 Fernando de Herrera (1534-97) v. p. 48

orally, on *pliegos sueltos* (broadsides), and in *romanceros* or *cancioneros*. Some are found in *cancioneros* of chapter III; but the flood of big collections began only about 1550: *Cancionero sin año* (of Antwerp, shortly before 1550); *Silva de varios romances* (1550). This most popular form of Spanish poetry spread with the Spanish language (colonies and Jews), and continues to be popular in Spanish literature. Other popular or folk lyric forms were cultivated (*villancicos, coplas*). All this in the face of the tidal wave of Classic tradition in the Renascence!

> Rom-Nav., pp. 75–80; Northup, ch. 12; Mer-Mor., pp. 171–180.

**X. Drama.** Secularization begins. Schools of Encina and Torres Naharro develop. Influence of the Celestina (XI, B) is seen.

A. Juan del Encina (1468?–1529?). Had a good musical training, and resided awhile in Rome. His popular *Cancionero* (1496) contains eight dramas, various verses, and his *Arte de la poesía castellana*. He initiated secularization of the drama, but still used much religious material. He used the ballad meter extensively. He wrote excellent lyrics and inserted many in his dramas. His use of the *sayagués* dialect (of country folk near Salamanca) in his *églogas* became a convention in later pastorals. He is called the father of the Spanish drama, for he is the earliest important dramatist known in Spain.

1. *Auto del repelón* (first appeared in the 1509 edition of his *Cancionero*). A comic farce of a brawl between Salamanca students and shepherds.
2. Italianate plays. In his *Égloga de Plácida y Vitoriano* (1513?) Plácida, after suicide, is revived for her lover by Venus and Mercury. In his *Égloga de Cristino y Febea* (written before 1514) the love of the nymph Febea wins the shepherd Cristino away from a hermit's life.
3. Christmas and Resurrection plays.

B. Bartolomé de Torres Naharro (died 1524?). Resided in Italy. His collected dramas were published under the title of *Propaladia*, "first fruits of Pallas," in Naples (1517). This volume also contains various poems,

Jacob Grimm – <u>Silva de romances viejos</u>
(Vienna, 1815) 69 best Spanish ballads

Lockhart – <u>Ancient Spanish Ballads</u>.
London, 1823. Most extensive translation
to English.

Durán. <u>Romancero general</u>, 5 vols. 1828-49.
Vols. X and XVI of BAE.
Extensive but not discriminating.

Wolf. <u>Primavera y flor de romances</u>.
(Berlin, 1856). Most scholarly collection.


all in verse
studied under Nebrija

Early Drama:
    Gómez Manrique – <u>Representación del
    nacimiento de nuestro Señor</u>.
        Earliest known drama after Reyes
                                        magos.
    Diego Sánchez de Badajoz – farsas, 1525-
                                            47


knew Encina in Rome

especially fine ballads and lyrics, and an important prologue
giving his dramatic theories: division into five acts; no
mention of the unities; observance of decorum. He says
there are two kinds of plays: *a noticia,* of real things;
and *a fantasía,* of things imagined, but with appearance of
truth. He amplified the secularization and versification
of Encina, and developed the *gracioso.* He was a master of
verse, and was the best satirist of his day. He was more
original than Encina, and his influence on later drama
was considerable.

*6 to 12 characters*

1. *Comedia Himenea.* The impetuous lover is forgiven by
   the girl's brother when his matrimonial intentions are
   made clear. This, his best, is the first cape and sword
   play and has remarkable character and plot development.
2. *Comedia Serafina.* The impetuous lover plans to kill
   his sweetheart in favor of a former love; but his brother
   loves his sweetheart, and the catastrophe is avoided.
3. *Comedia Tinelaria.* Satirizes corruption and intrigue
   through discussions in the *tinelo,* or servants' mess hall,
   of a Roman palace.
4. *Comedia Soldadesca.* A realistic portrayal of soldier life.
   (1 and 2 are *comedias a fantasía;* 3 and 4 are *comedias a
   noticia.*)

C. GIL VICENTE (1470?–1536?). Was official court playwright
   and creator of the drama in Portugal. He wrote 11 plays in
   Castilian, 16 in Portuguese, and the remainder of his 44 in a
   mixture of the two. He began with Encina as a model.
   Allegory and symbolism are prominent, and lyric poetry is
   aptly interspersed. He had roots in the folk, but flowered in
   the court.

*musician*

1. [*Auto da barca do Inferno, Auto da barca do Purgatorio*],
   *Auto da barca da Gloria* (1517, 1518, 1519). The first
   two of this trilogy are in Portuguese; the last is in
   Castilian. They sing again the grim Dance of Death
   theme (see II, C), and constitute this period's finest
   contribution to the morality play.
2. *Auto da Sibila Casandra* (1509?). Written in Castilian.
   This shepherdess believes herself to be the virgin to
   bear Christ, but the real Nativity scene is disclosed at

arte mayor with hemistich ( pie que-
                                      brado )

the end.   A recitation of the fifteen signs of Judgment
Day is awe inspiring.

3. *Comedia do viuvo* (1514).   Written in Castilian.   This is
a wedding play in which two brothers marry the two
daughters of a widower.

4. *Dom Duardos* (1525) and *Amadís de Gaula* (1533).
The first plays in Spanish based on romances of chivalry.
*Dom Duardos* is based on *Palmerín de Oliva*.   See V, B
and XI, A.

D. LOPE DE RUEDA (1510?–1565).   Of Sevilla, a typical *autor*
(author-manager) of a traveling company, writing new
plays and adapting old plays (many Italian).   His collected
works were published by Timoneda (in 1567–1570).   Most
of his plays are in prose, which was rare before the 19th
century.   He is most famed for his *pasos*.   He developed
stock characters with conventional names, mostly native
types: the *bobo*, barber, cleric, braggart soldier, etc.   His
style is vigorous, vivid, and direct.   Cervantes admired and
was influenced by him, and his imitators are numerous.   He
brought the drama from the palace and Church out into
the market place, and educated the people to a popular
drama.

> *Pasos* (written around the mid-16th century).   Short
> prose sketches or farces with a slight plot.   Good
> examples are: *Las aceitunas, Los lacayos ladrones,
> Cornudo y contento*.

> Rom-Nav., pp. 109–119, 194–200;  Northup, pp. 232–239;
> Mer-Mor., pp. 143–146, 207–215, 323–325;  J. P. W. Craw-
> ford: *Spanish drama before Lope de Vega*, chs. 2–6;  J. P. W.
> Crawford: *Spanish pastoral drama* (Philadelphia 1915).

XI. **Novel.**   There developed in the Renascence a new or novel
type, growing out of material in Chapters II and V.

A. CHIVALRIC.   Originated anonymously as 14th century
prosifications of late epics, recreated as a pure novel form
(see V, B).   This type flowered in the Renascence and
withered in the Golden Age.   The chivalric fad coincided
with the marvelous adventure stories of New World ex-
plorers.   These exotic yarns were the dime novels of the
day.   They were all the rage, from lowest to highest:
*Francis I of France (ruled 1515–1547), St. Ignatius of

\* had *Amadís* trans. to Fr. — had become
acquainted with it while Sp. prisoner
(1525–26)

Plays: Eufemia in 8 "scenas"
Armelina in 6 "scenas"

Loyola (1491–1556), and St. Teresa (XVI, B) devoured them with zeal. Editions, sequels, translations, and imitations multiplied rapidly throughout Europe.

1. *Amadís de Gaula* cycle. The earliest allusion to Amadís is in Spain (see V, B, 6). The only preserved version is that of Garci Rodríguez de Montalvo, *Los cuatro libros del virtuoso caballero Amadís de Gaula* (1508), in clear, florid, Renascence prose. Montalvo probably wrote the fourth book only. This work exerted a great influence on the manners and imagination of the period (chivalric virtue and ideas on love, bravery, sacrifice, fair play, fidelity), and portrayed the ideal and perfect knight. It is the best of the type. *Las sergas de Esplandián* (Amadís' son) (1510) is a long, independent novel, added as a fifth book to *Amadís*, and was probably written by Montalvo. The name of a fictitious island in *Esplandián* was bestowed on California.

2. *Palmerín* cycle. The chief rival of *Amadís;* flourished simultaneously. First of this cycle is *Palmerín de Oliva* (1511); second, *Primaleón* (1512), attributed to Francisco Vázquez de Ciudad Rodrigo. Greatest in the cycle is *Palmerín de Inglaterra* (1547–1548) [originally written in Portuguese by Francisco de Moraes in 1544, published in 1567].

3. *Tirant lo Blanc.* The first three parts are by Joannot Martorell, the fourth by John of Galba. It appeared [in Catalan in 1490] in Castilian translation in 1511. It is realistic, obscene, and burlesque. A duel in underwear and other rare episodes make this the first parody of the type.

Rom-Nav., pp. 97–100, 204–206; Northup, pp. 145–153; Mer-Mor., pp. 135–140, 195–198; W. J. Entwistle: *The Arthurian legend in the literatures of the Spanish peninsula* (New York 1925).

B. *Celestina* or *(Tragi-)Comedia de Calisto y Melibea.* The first preserved edition (1499) is of 16 acts, the 1502 edition of 21 acts, and the 1526 edition of 22 acts. The additional acts are inserted between original acts 14 and 15. An acrostic in the 1501 edition states Fernando de Rojas was the author. Written in the form of a drama, in prose, this work is meant only to be read. It tells of the tragic death

Last original novel of chivalry by
Juan de Silva, Don Policisne de
Boecia (1602)

of two lovers, brought together by a go-between (Celestina),
who represents the highest literary development of the
go-between type (see II, B, 2, *b*, Trotaconventos). Characterization is more important than plot. The type of
language is fitted to the character. The work abounds in
picaresque elements, proverbs, and other folk elements, and
is predominantly realistic. It shows the power of human
passion and of fate. Its chief sources are the Roman poet
Ovid (43 B.C.–17 A.D.) and the Italian poet Petrarch
(1304–1374), the Roman dramatists Plautus (died 184 B.C.)
and Terence (190?–159? B.C.), and the medieval Spanish
writers Juan Ruiz and Martínez de Toledo. The *Celestina*
exerted a great influence both on the novel and the drama.
Numerous editions (63 in 16th century Spain alone),
translations, and imitations (James Mabbe's *Spanish bawd*
of 1631 is important in English literature) appeared. The
*Celestina* is considered by many the second greatest work
in Spanish literature (after *Don Quijote*, XV, C, 1). Its
universality, classic eloquence, and brilliant style make it a
world masterpiece.

Rom-Nav., pp. 103–106; Northup, pp. 162–169; Mer-Mor.,
pp. 140–143.

C. SENTIMENTAL. Treats the love theme idealistically; often
contains veiled personal reminiscences, much allegory, and
defense of woman (the contrary of V, A, 3 and V, C, 2).
Italian influence, especially of Boccaccio (1313–1375), is
notable. Usually the ending is tragic. This type was
highly popular in its own day.

1. Juan Rodríguez de la Cámara or del Padrón (died about
   1450). Was probably a page of Juan II (see III, C).
   He wrote *El siervo libre de amor* (about 1440), based in
   part on Boccaccio's *Fiammetta* (written in the early
   1340's). It contains chivalric episodes and moralizing,
   and is the precursor of this type.
2. Diego de San Pedro (late 15th century). His *Cárcel de
   amor* (1492), after relating many amorous adventures,
   intermingling fancy with the author's own memories, a
   eulogy of women, and much allegory, concludes with
   the hero's suicide. Lord Berners' English translation
   (about 1540) is an early monument of Euphuism. San
   Pedro's popular novel, chiefly in the form of letters.

Petrarch, De remediis utriosque
fortunae

Verse work Triunfs de los donos
refutes
Boccaccio's Corbaccio

became the breviary of the lovelorn, and is the best of this type.

3. *Cuestión de amor* (about 1510). Composed anonymously in Naples, where the scene is laid. It is in mingled prose and verse, and presents real personages veiled. It is the best of the many imitations of the *Cárcel de amor*.

4. Juan de Flores about 1495 published *Grimalte y Gradisa*, an incoherent continuation of Boccaccio's *Fiammetta;* and *Grisel y Mirabella*, along the lines of the medieval dispute type (II, A, 2), with a violent tragic ending.

Rom-Nav., pp. 100–103; Northup, p. 157; Mer-Mor., pp. 117–118, 133–135, 198.

**XII. Didactic literature.** See VII, A and B for Humanism.

A. HISTORY.

1. National.

(a) Diego de Valera (1412–1487?). His *Crónica de España* (1482), called *Crónica abreviada*, is an uncritical fusion of fact and fiction, complementing the *Crónica de don Juan II* (written about the mid-15th century by several collaborators; Juan II ruled 1406–1454).

(b) Hernando del Pulgar (1436?–1492). Official chronicler of Fernando and Isabel (ruled jointly 1474–1504). His *Claros varones de Castilla* (1486) is a collection of biographies of great figures of Enrique IV's (ruled 1454–1474) court.

(c) Florián de Ocampo (1499?–1558). Printed a late (third) version of Alfonso X's *Crónica general* of Spain (VI, B, 2) in 1541. This was the only current form of this chronicle for more than 300 years, and was the popular source of information on epic stories for writers during that time.

Rom-Nav., pp. 88–89, 172–173; Northup, pp. 77, 79, 216; Mer-Mor., pp. 129–133, 181–182.

2. American. Spain's discovery, exploration, and conquest of the New World, and her establishment of an American colonial empire gave occasion for many histories.

(a) Bartolomé de las Casas (1474–1566). His *Historia general de las Indias* (written 1552–1561, but not published till 1875–1876) covers the period 1492–

"novela de clave" (Benedetto Croce
identified some of the characters)


Pedro de Corral                        , Crónica
sarracina or Crónica del rey don
Rodrigo con la destrucción de España
(1440) "first historical novel!"


[1525] Oviedo, De la historia
natural de las Indias

1520, and is the most popular source book for the
early period. His *Destrucción de las Indias* (published
1552, but written many years earlier) defends the
noble savage against bad treatment by the conquerors.

(b) Hernando Cortés (1485–1547). Conquered Mexico
(1519–1521). In five *Cartas de relación*, written to
Carlos V (ruled 1516–1556) during 1522-1524, he
gives a vivid account of his conquests. See XVII,
A, 2, b.

(c) Álvaro Núñez Cabeza de Vaca (1507?–1559?). His
*Naufragios* (1542) vividly describes his shipwrecks
and explorations in the Gulf States (during 1527–
1536).

Rom-Nav., p. 173; Northup, pp. 150, 204–207; Mer-Mor.,
pp. 182–185.

B. REFORMATION. Within the Church and of the religious
orders in Spain. The Jesuit order was founded in 1540.
Erasmus (1467–1536) had many followers in Spain. There
was no serious persecution of literary men by the Inquisition
except some Salamanca scholars suspected of being Jews.
The Church was still the greatest patron of literature: many
great 16th century men of letters served it; a great body
of literature by the Mystics, which budded in the Renascence and flowered in the Golden Age and contains some
of the finest specimens of 16th century literature, sprang
from the Church and some of its most ardent reformers.
With the Council of Trent (1545–1563) and its dampening,
quieting influence, the age of rebirth, exuberance, and rapid
growth ends, and there appear, in the reign of Felipe II
(ruled 1556–1598), the concentrated, refining processes of
the Golden Age of Spanish literature.


## GOLDEN AGE

Mer-Mor., pp. 149–159, 216–220, 365–370; Chapman, chs.
23–30.

### XIII. Poetry.

A. LYRIC. Of the earlier part of the period (late 16th century),
before Gongorism, divides into two schools: Castilian and
Andalusian.

Seville                                          S alamanca

1. Luis Ponce de León (1527–1591). Associated with the Mystics (XVI, D). He is most representative of the Castilian school, which is calm and simple in taste, clear and exact in expression. He wrote only some thirty original poems, besides translations from the Bible and the Classics. He expresses genuine human emotion with sobriety and austerity. His *Vida retirada* and *Noche serena* are as fine as any lyrics ever written. His works circulated in manuscript, and finally were published by Quevedo (XV, B, 7) in 1631 to counteract Gongorism (XIII, D). He is the greatest poet of the early Golden Age.

   A. F. G. Bell: *Luis de León* (Oxford 1925).

2. Fernando de Herrera (1534?–1597). Called "el Divino." He was the leader of the Andalusian school, which is imaginative and subtle in expression, and rich in figures of speech. He was best known in his day for his love lyrics, mostly sonnets, in Neoplatonic Italian fashion. He anticipated *culteranismo* (XIII, D). In expression and manner he is brusque, vigorous, and independent. In emotion he is tender, deep, and spiritual. Famed for his odes, especially *De la batalla naval de Lepanto* (1572), he best attains a lofty patriotism and noble style in them. From the Bible, Latin, and Italian he enriched poetic vocabulary and elevated style.

   Rom-Nav., pp. 144–153, 158–163; Northup, pp. 140–144; Mer-Mor., pp. 221–227, 235–241, 253–255.

B. BALLAD. See Chapter IX. The *romances artísticos* particularly belong to this period. A grand collection of them was made in the *Romancero general* (1600). In the 17th century *romanceros* on special heroes or subjects appeared. From that time on the *romances vulgares* have been widely cultivated; a famous collection of them is Juan Hidalgo's *Romances de germanía* (1609). Góngora (XIII, D, 2) and Quevedo (XIII, D, 3) wrote excellent *romances*, which enjoyed wide popularity.

   Rom-Nav., see again pp. 75–80; Northup, see again ch. 12, especially pp. 216–217, 347, 395; Mer-Mor., see again pp. 171–180, 496.

translated from Virgil : Eclogues
I, II, III, IV, thru X
Georgics I + II
Horace 26 odes some
in several versions
Pindar, Tibullus one ode
each

C. ERUDITE EPIC. Very popular among Golden Age writers because: the epic ranked high in the Classics; a great Renascence Italian epic tradition set the fashion; need of epic expression was felt, inspired by the great national pride of a world-conquering people and by profound religious sentiment of the champion nation of Catholicism in its hour of need. Besides history and religion, rich imagination, the Classics, and burlesques inspired epics. Their usual form was the *octava real* (see VIII, A, 1). Quick to flower and quick to wither, unlike the medieval folk epic (II, A, 1), this poetry has little in common with the interests of our age.

1. Historic. Includes the best epics of this period.

   (*a*) National. Bernardo de Balbuena's (1568–1625?) *Bernardo* (1624) celebrates the victory of Roncesvalles (see II, A, 1, *b* and *c*), and is Spain's best Golden Age epic after the *Araucana*.

   (*b*) American. Alonso de Ercilla y Zúñiga's (1533–1594) *Araucana* (1569–1589), on the insurrection of the Araucanian Indians in Chile against their Spanish conquerors, intermingles fantastic love and miscellaneous episodes with an idealization of the Indian. The author actually participated in the struggle and gives the vivid description of an eyewitness. This is the best Golden Age epic.

2. Romantic. Lope de Vega's (XIV, C) *Hermosura de Angélica* (1602) and *Jerusalén conquistada* (1609).

3. Religious. Cristóbal de Virués' (1550–1609?) *Monserrate* (1587).

4. Classic themes. Lope de Vega's *Andrómeda* (1621).

5. Burlesque. José de Villaviciosa's (1589–1658) *Mosquea* (1615) sings of the deeds of flies; and Lope de Vega's *Gatomaquia* (1634) of cat love.

   Rom-Nav., pp. 163–166, 210, 310; Northup, pp. 228–230; Mer-Mor., pp. 241–253, 293.

D. GONGORISM. Broke out in Spain in the late Golden Age (17th century), marking the beginning of decadence, along with satire. Although Gongorism means frequently *culteranismo*, it is an inseparable combination of: (1) *conceptismo* or subtlety of thought or wit, finespun argumentation on questions of love and honor, expressed in rhetorical

Best in peninsula : Luis Camões
(1524?-1580), Os Lusíadas (1572)

terms (abundance of figures of speech, especially the *concepto*, " conceit" and *equívoco*, " wordplay"); and (2) *culteranismo* or cultivation of obscurity in expression or style, with display of erudition (abundance of Classic and mythological allusions, extreme Latinization of vocabulary and syntax). Both tendencies exist in literature at all times, but in the 17th century their combined excessive cultivation became a craze which clothed thought and expression in mazes so intricate that none could understand them. It penetrated all forms of literature, and persisted well into the 18th century. The chief contribution of Gongorism was enrichment of vocabulary and imagery.

1. Luis de Carrillo y Sotomayor (1583?-1610). His *Libro de la erudición poética* (1607) expounds doctrines of Gongorism, which Carrillo put into practice in his poems published in 1611.
2. Luis de Góngora y Argote (1561-1627). Of Andalusia, began with popular songs and ballads, in the tradition of Herrera, excelling in *letrillas* and brilliant satire, which show him at his best. But his *Panegírico al duque de Lerma* (1609) shows him turning to adopt Carrillo's theories, chiefly *culteranismo*. His *Fábula de Polifemo y Galatea* (1613?), *Soledades* (1613?), and *Fábula de Píramo y Tisbe* (1618) are perfect examples of obscurity. Góngora was the greatest poet of the late Golden Age.
3. Quevedo. Most important in the picaresque novel (XV, B, 7), he was nevertheless one of the most prolific lyric poets of his day (see XIII, B). He wrote every type and quality of verse. Gongorism, chiefly *conceptismo*, satire, wit, and didacticism characterize his poetry.

   Rom-Nav., ch. 22, pp. 289-292; Northup, pp. 294-303, 304-306; Mer-Mor., pp. 227-235, 237-238; E. K. Kane: *Gongorism and the Golden Age* (Chapel Hill 1928).

**XIV. Drama.** The drama and picaresque novel are the livest types in the Golden Age. A Spanish national drama was outlined in the Renascence by Lope de Rueda, formulated in the Golden Age by Juan de la Cueva, and perfected by the four great stars: Lope de Vega, Calderón, Tirso, and Alarcón.

A. JUAN DE LA CUEVA (1543-1610). Of Sevilla, wrote considerable poetry. His *Ejemplar poético* (1606) formulated

*theater also flourished in Valencia*

At first there were other dramatists
cultivating the classical tragedy:
    Juan de Mal Lara        Cristobel
                                de Virués
                              (1550-1609)

the theory of the Golden Age national drama; reduced the number of acts from five to four; recommended a rich variety of verse forms (native and Italian); ignored the unities of time and place, and other hampering pseudo-Aristotelian rules; and, most important, it recommended the use of national themes from Spanish history and tradition, found in the chronicles and *romanceros*. Cueva had practiced this precept in some of his own dramas: *Siete infantes de Lara* (1579), *Bernardo del Carpio* (1579) (see II, A, 1, *c* and *e*), and *Saco de Roma* (1579), an event which occurred in 1527. Thus he would appeal to the whole nation rather than to a particular class. He produced in all fourteen dramas in Sevilla between 1579 and 1581, basing several on historic subjects, using the supernatural and sensational, and introducing the epico-lyric character of the ballad into the drama. His *Infamador* (1581) is considered by some a model for Tirso's *Burlador de Sevilla* (XIV, F, 1). Cueva is remembered more for his theories than for his dramas.

B. CERVANTES. This master of the novel (XV, C) aspired to dramatic fame in the 1580's, and was keenly disappointed when Lope de Vega eclipsed him. But he persisted till the end, and published *Ocho comedias y ocho entremeses nuevos, nunca representados* (1615), some really new, others reworked. He could create characters and lively dialogue, but he lacked dramatic sense. His patriotic *Numancia*, with some impressive, tragic scenes, celebrates a siege in lofty style. *Pedro de Urdemalas* is gypsy and picaresque, as its name of Spain's traditional folklore hero suggests. The *Trato de Argel* and *Baños de Argel* are Moorish, and may be reminiscent of Cervantes' captivity in Africa. Best are his *entremeses: La guarda cuidadosa, La cueva de Salamanca, El viejo celoso*, displaying his broadly sympathetic, human, and humorous traits.

C. LOPE FÉLIX DE VEGA CARPIO (1562–1635). Spain's greatest dramatic genius was born in Madrid. His earliest play, *El verdadero amante*, was said to have been written at the age of twelve. After a casual education and a tumultuous life, he was ordained a priest (1614). This extremely prolific master improvisor (more than 400 dramas preserved and many more lost) boasted that he averaged twenty sheets of writing a day all his life. His novels are

Best writer of entremeses : Quiñones
de Benavente (     -1651)

mostly forgotten (see XV, A, 4).  He excels as a lyric poet,
and figures prominently in the erudite epic (XIII, C, 2, 4,
and 5).  His dramas, which he regarded as hack work,
overshadow his other works.  His *Comedias* were published
in twenty-five volumes (1604–1647), and haphazardly ever
since; some are of doubtful authenticity.  In his *Arte
nuevo de hacer comedias en este tiempo* (1609), Lope says the
*vulgo*, or common people, who do not understand art, pay
him, hence he writes not art, but what the *vulgo* can understand.  He says the drama should mingle tragedy and
comedy, as well as metrical forms, for the *vulgo* likes
action and variety.  Indeed, Lope realistically portrays
true, natural life and passion in his dramas.  Only unity of
action should be kept, says he.  Language should fit character.  Verisimilitude should be observed.  These ideas
derive mostly from Italian critics.  Lope himself specified:
the number of acts should be three; the climax should come
in the middle of the third act; subtle devices should be used
(" deceiving with the truth," wordplay, etc.).  *Pundonor*
becomes the chief motivating force.  Lope's fine ability to
spot a dramatic situation was instinctive.  He exploited a
huge store of plots, and often repeated.  Careless but
graceful and appropriate in style, he made some concession
to the prevailing taste for *conceptismo*.  *El mejor alcalde el
rey* is a typical Lope play.  His dramas should be viewed as
a panoramic whole rather than individually.

1. *Comedias de capa y espada.*  These purely Spanish,
   complex love and honor intrigues of the aristocracy and
   middle-class life and manners show him at his best.
2. *Autos sacramentales.*  Lope was good in this type of
   religious allegory, but Calderón was the best (see
   XIV, H, 3).
3. *Comedias históricas.*  Based on chronicles and ballads,
   especially national themes, and romances of chivalry.
4. *Comedias de carácter.*  Feature some social type.
5. *Comedias mitológicas, pastoriles, picarescas, de santos.*
6. *Loas* and *entremeses.*
7. Novelistic plots and various inventions of his own.

D. AGUSTÍN DE ROJAS VILLANDRANDO (1572–1612?).  His
*Viaje entretenido* (1603) describes practical conditions of the
contemporary theater, the earliest Madrid theaters and

Fuente ovejuna
Peribáñez y el comendador de Ocaña
La moza del cántaro
El castigo sin venganza
La noche Toledana
El remedio en la desdicha
La dama boba
El villano en su rincón
Amar sin saber a quién.




La estrella de Sevilla (?)




Antonio Mira de Amescua (1574?-1644?)
     El esclavo del demonio
     Judía de Toledo (subject
                         treated by Lope)

their physical arrangement, actors and their life, and the manner of circulation of plays. Rojas was the best writer of his time of *loas* (prologues, often praising the actors and flattering the audience). Many *loas* are scattered through his *Viaje entretenido.*

E. GUILLÉN DE CASTRO Y BELLVÍS (1569–1631). The most famous of the Valencian group. The latter part of his life was spent in Madrid. He published two volumes (1618 and 1625), containing twelve plays each, and various other plays, totaling about fifty in all. He was the first to dramatize the Cid legend (from ballads): *Mocedades del Cid* (1618) develops the conflict of love and honor in Jimena (who becomes the Cid's wife), and is the direct source of Corneille's *Cid* (1636); *Hazañas del Cid* (1618) tells of the siege of Zamora and other youthful adventures of the Cid (see II, A, 1, *h*). Castro dramatized plots taken from Cervantes; also from ballads, as in his *Conde Alarcos* (1618). He was an admirer and imitator of Lope de Vega. He followed traditions established by Cueva. He liked intricate plots and emotional conflicts.

F. GABRIEL TÉLLEZ (pen name, Tirso de Molina) (1583?–1648). This rival and follower of Lope de Vega was born in Madrid. He wrote more than 400 dramas, of which only about 80 are preserved. His first collection, called *Cigarrales de Toledo* (1621), contains three dramas, various prose and verse. Another of the several collections published during his lifetime, *Deleitar aprovechando* (1632), contains three *autos*, verses, and three novels. Both these collections have frames, and contain his dramatic theories, mostly agreeing with and praising Lope de Vega's ideas: write for the *vulgo*, and disregard hampering rules. A confessor, he had a sympathetic understanding of various temperaments. Best are his women characters and *graciosos*.

1. *El burlador de Sevilla y convidado de piedra* (1630). This, Tirso's masterpiece, gave don Juan Tenorio to world literature. Thousands of artistic works are based on this play, notably Molière's French drama, *Festin de Pierre* (1665), the opera *Don Giovanni* (1787) by the Austrian composer Mozart, and the English poem *Don Juan* (1819–1824), last and greatest work of Byron. This is one of the best, and certainly the most widely

Luis Vélez de Guevara (1579-1644) [see p. 74]
In addition to _El diablo cojuelo_ (1641)
wrote perhaps 400 comedias (80 preserved)
among which _Reinar después de morir_, o
_Doña Inés de Castro_ and _Más pesa_
_el rey que la sangre_ — story of Guzmán
el bueno who allows Moors to kill
his son rather than surrender Tarifa
to them. One of best 2$^{nd}$ rank dramatists, called " Quitapesares " by Cervantes
for his gaiety & animation.

known cape and sword play. Tirso's don Juan is the finest in character.

2. *El condenado por desconfiado* (1635). Tirso's best and one of Spain's best religious plays. Unfortunately his authorship of this and the preceding play has been doubted. Its thesis is the importance of faith and repentance.

3. *La prudencia en la mujer* (1633). María de Molina, regent of Fernando IV (ruled 1295-1312), circumvents intrigues and keeps the throne for her son. This is Tirso's best historical play.

4. *Los amantes de Teruel* (1635). Based on the folk legend of this Romeo and Juliet of Spain (see XXIV, A, 4, *a*).

5. *El vergonzoso en palacio* (1621). A bashful courtier is wooed by a woman who is not so bashful. This is one of Tirso's best character portrayals.

G. JUAN RUIZ DE ALARCÓN Y MENDOZA (1581?-1639). A Mexican hunchback and a business man. His plays (published in two parts, 1628 and 1634) are finished products and small in number (about twenty). He developed a thesis through a typical character, a method taken over by great French dramatists like Corneille (1606-1684) and Molière (1622-1673). He was the greatest writer of thesis plays (which illustrate moral truths through a character type), and best polisher of this period.

1. *La verdad sospechosa* (1619?). The fate of a youth who cultivates lying as an art shows us that liars should have good memories. This play was adapted by Corneille in *Le menteur* (1642).

2. *Las paredes oyen* (before 1622). Attacks slander.

3. *Mudarse por mejorarse* (before 1622). Attacks inconstancy in love.

H. PEDRO CALDERÓN DE LA BARCA HENAO DE LA BARRERA Y RIAÑO (1600-1681). Spain's most polished dramatist was born in Madrid. He ruled the Spanish stage for more than half a century (mid and late 17th), and his influence extended well into the 18th century. Romanticists in the early 19th century gave him first place in the Spanish drama; now he must share honors with Lope de Vega. He had a fine education in theology and law. In 1651 he was ordained a priest, and after that wrote only for the court

Marta la piadosa
Don Gil de las calzas verdes

No hay mal que por bien no venga
El tejedor de Segovia (part II)
Los favores del mundo

and *autos*. He wrote little except drama. He was naturally influenced somewhat by the new fad of Gongorism (XIII, D). Lope de Vega's was a drama of passion; Calderón's of thought. Lope was fresh and real; Calderón planned solemnly and intelligently a theater of ideas: honor, monarchy, religion. He wrote, besides over 100 full-length dramas, several *entremeses* and minor types. He excelled in the cape and sword play and *auto*. He could reduce a play to a polished gem of clear, swift action, with precise and simple outline.

*[handwritten margin note: 120 comedias / 80 autos]*

1. *La vida es sueño* (1635). Portrays the conflict of fate and free will. Reason shows this life to be an illusory dream; real truth lies in the life beyond. The symbolic character of the hero, Segismundo, shows how man can dominate his material self. This philosophic play is Calderón's masterpiece.
2. *El mágico prodigioso* (1637). From the legend of St. Cyprian of Antioch's (4th century) pact with the Devil, similar to the Faust theme and to Mira de Amescua's *Esclavo del demonio* (1612). This is Calderón's best religious play.
3. *Autos sacramentales.* Short allegorical plays in praise of the Eucharist or mystery of the Holy Sacrament, played on *carros* in plazas on Corpus Christi day (Thursday after Trinity Sunday, which is the eighth Sunday after Easter). Calderón esteemed most highly his seventy odd *autos;* indeed, he is the best writer of this type, for his imagination and lyric splendor find most brilliant outlet in them.

*[handwritten margin note: performance prohibited in 1765]*

4. *El príncipe constante* (1629). Deals with the early 15th century prince Fernando of Portugal, who sacrificed liberty and life for patriotism and religion.
5. *Comedias de capa y espada.* As *La dama duende* (1629), *Casa con dos puertas mala es de guardar* (1629), *Guárdate del agua mansa* (Still water runs deep) (1649). With intricate plots of love and honor, these all follow the same general pattern, and offer a good picture of the extravagant ideals of that age.
6. *El alcalde de Zalamea* (1651). Has excellent characterization, and is the best of his series of tragedies on *pundonor:* as *El médico de su honra* (1635), *A secreto agravio secreta venganza* (1635), etc.

I. FRANCISCO DE ROJAS ZORRILLA (1607–1648). Published two volumes of his plays (1640 and 1645). He developed a new type, the *comedia de gracioso*, with a fool as the chief character. His style is sometimes clear, sometimes clouded with Gongorism, at times hasty. He was imitated extensively by French dramatists. His masterpiece, *Del rey abajo ninguno*, unjustly overshadows his minor plays: *Entre bobos anda el juego* or *Don Lucas del cigarral* (1638), *Donde hay agravios no hay celos, y amo criado* (1637), *No hay ser padre siendo rey* (1635).

*1ˢᵗ comedia de figurón* [handwritten margin note]

> *Del rey abajo ninguno* or *El labrador más honrado García del Castañar* (1650). Still quite popular in Spain, this play is a striking example of the honor theme, with gripping action, lyric tone, and intense conflict of passion.

J. AGUSTÍN MORETO Y CAVAÑA (1618–1669). Practically ceased his dramatic work when he became a priest in 1657. He published a volume of his plays in 1654. Two more volumes appeared in 1676 and 1681. He often reworked his earlier plays and those of others, and frequently improved his originals with his excellent finishing art. He is simple and clear in style and plot, classic in taste, witty and jovial in tone. He created fine *comedias de figurón* (caricatures).

1. *El desdén con el desdén* (1654). Fused earlier plots of Lope de Vega and Tirso into a brilliant gem of live comedy. A haughty young lady is finally humbled by her haughtier suitor. This play, imitated by Molière in *La princesse d'Élide* (1664), is Moreto's masterpiece.
2. *El lindo don Diego* (1662). The caricature of a dude, one of the best *comedias de figurón*.
3. *El valiente justiciero* (1657). Is a successful reworking of the *Infanzón de Illescas* (1633; by Tirso ?) on the legend of how Pedro el Cruel (ruled 1350–1369) brought to earth the vanity of a haughty noble. This is one of Spain's finest historical dramas.

Rom-Nav., pp. 200–202, 230, 241–246, chs. 24–28; Northup, pp. 187–188, 239–243, ch. 16, pp. 306–311; Mer-Mor., pp. 300–302, 325–364, 372–389; J. P. W. Crawford: *Spanish drama before Lope de Vega*, chs. 7–8; H. J. Chaytor: *Dramatic theory in Spain* (Cambridge 1925).

Del rey abajo ninguno called by
M y P the most modern S. de O. play
in structure. Can be performed without
"refundición"

**XV. Novel.** Reached its apex in the early 17th century, and exerted a wide influence over Europe. The novel developed into various modern types and, in most cases, the greatest example of each type was produced.

A. PASTORAL. The most popular type born in the late 16th century, just after the novel of chivalry began to wane. Boccaccio's *Ameto* (1341), in Italian, was the first pastoral novel to mingle prose and verse: pastoral poems are the jewels in a setting of prose which carries the thread of the story. Sannazaro's *Arcadia* (1504) imitated the *Ameto*, and is the great Italian model for the type in Spain and subsequently in northern Europe. The tradition of the Classic eclogue was already found in Spanish Renascence poetry and drama; now it was adopted by the novel and developed into a pattern so highly conventionalized that originality soon faded out. The characters represent real persons of the day in shepherd disguise; local interest was enlivened by timely allusions. Magic and supernatural elements abound. Plots are slight.

1. Jorge de Montemayor (1520?–1561). A Portuguese musician who lived in Spain, traveled in Italy, and knew Spanish and Italian poetry well. His *Diana* (about 1559), with a slight plot of a love triangle, and musical verses interspersed among charming prose episodes, enjoyed an enormous success in its day, both in Spain and abroad: in England Philip Sidney's *Arcadia* (1590) and Shakespeare's *Two Gentlemen of Verona* (1595), and in France Honoré d'Urfé's *Astrée* (1607–1624) are indebted to Montemayor. He is also noted for his poetry, both native and Italian style. His *Diana* is the first and best Spanish pastoral.

2. Gaspar Gil Polo's *Diana enamorada* (1564). Solves the love triangle developed by Montemayor. Mediocre in plot, excellent in style, its poetic pieces are classic. It is the best of the many sequels to Montemayor's *Diana*.

3. Cervantes' (XV, C) *Galatea* (1585). Is modeled on the *Dianas*. The characters represent real persons, but lack individuality. A second part was promised but never appeared. Cervantes labored over and polished this work more than any other, entrusting his fame to it. It was his first important published work.

Tasso (1544-95) Aminta
Guarini (1537-1612) Il Pastor Fido
(1585) pastoral drama


Bernadim Ribeiro (1482?-1552)
Saudades ou menina e
moça (1554, II 1557)
[also has chivalric elements]

4. Lope de Vega's (XIV, C) *Arcadia* (1598). Allusions center about the author (Belardo) and the duke of Alba (Anfriso). The work is based on the *Dianas* and follows the pastoral pattern closely. It shows poetic genius.

Rom-Nav., pp. 206–211, 246–248, 308–309; Northup, pp. 153–157; Mer-Mor., pp. 199–201, 289–294.

B. PICARESQUE. The word *picaro* (a ragged street urchin or rogue) is found first in 1548. *Picaros* were usually porters, errand boys, or personal servants, not above petty crime, and living by their wits. They became a recognized social class. Picaresque elements appear in poetry and drama, but attain their best literary expression in the novel, which realistically portrays the life of a wandering rogue who serves masters typical of various social classes, which are satirized as seen through the rogue's eyes, within their own homes, with varying amounts of moralizing, often parodying chivalric novels. Picaresque novels are usually autobiographic, and have no unity except the rogue's personality. Sometimes a female rogue, a soul (as in Antonio Enríquez Gómez's *Siglo pitagórico*, 1644), an animal, or even a coin passing from owner to owner varies the pattern. Pedro de Urdemalas, Spanish folk-tale hero, is a rogue type. The picaresque novels were widely translated and imitated through Europe. The two best types of Spanish novel are the picaresque and regional (XXV, C).

1. Francisco Delicado (early 16th century). This Andalusian priest wrote *La lozana andaluza* (Venice 1528). Corruption in Rome is described. The vocabulary is rich and colloquial. This is the earliest preserved picaresque novel.

2. *Lazarillo de Tormes*. Anonymous (may be by Diego Hurtado de Mendoza). Three editions in 1554 are the earliest preserved, but Lazarillo was known earlier, perhaps in oral circulation. The hero tells of his birth, childhood, service of seven masters (blind beggar, priest, gentleman, friar, indulgence seller, chaplain, constable), and finally of his marriage and settling down as town crier of Toledo. The work is profoundly human, with keen satire and boldly realistic sketches of life. It

*[margin note: slangs, characters influenced by Celestina]*

*[margin note: chapters = tratados]*

Chapter called "marmotretos," — in
dialogue — contains Italian, Catalan +
broken Spanish

<u>Continuation</u> by Juan de la Luna
in Paris (1620)

has enjoyed an enormous popularity, and is the best, as
well as one of the earliest, of the type.

3. Mateo Alemán (1547–1614?). Son of a Sevillian prison
doctor, he learned much about rogues in childhood.
Long a government clerk in Madrid, he finally went to
Mexico. About a fifty-year gap intervened between
*Lazarillo* and Alemán's masterpiece, *Guzmán de Alfarache.* Is this due to censorship? The first part of
*Guzmán* (1599) went through fifteen editions in fifteen
years (more popular than *Don Quijote* in the same
period). A spurious second part appeared in 1602, by
the Valencian lawyer Martí. The genuine second part
appeared in 1604. A Sevillian rogue tells of his wander-
ings through Spain and Italy, with much moralizing,
many stories, proverbs, and keen observations on life.
After *Lazarillo*, *Guzmán* is the best of this type.

4. *La pícara Justina* (1605). By Francisco López de
Úbeda (may be a pen name). This female rogue tricks
her lovers. The second part, in which she was to marry
Guzmán de Alfarache, never appeared. Every episode
begins with a verse summary and ends with a moral.

5. Vicente Espinel (1550–1624). This adventurer simply
tells of his own life in his *Marcos de Obregón* (1618),
mingled with various episodes. Moralizing at the end
praises patience. Lesage's *Gil Blas* (see XXII, B, 2)
owes much to *Marcos.*

6. Cervantes (XV, C) contributed to the picaresque novel,
especially in his *Novelas ejemplares* (1613): *Coloquio
de los perros*, in which one dog tells another about his
masters, with typical Cervantine mild satire of social
classes; and *Rinconete y Cortadillo*, two boys who join
a rogues' union in Sevilla.

7. Francisco Gómez de Quevedo y Villegas (1580–1645).
Born in Madrid, Quevedo was a wealthy courtier and a
literary genius of first rank, along with Cervantes and
Lope de Vega. He rebelled at court corruption, which
he knew well. His sharp tongue got him into prison.
He was a great stylist and better educated than Cervantes, but lacked the latter's sense of balance. His
work is marred by Gongorism, although he preached
against it (see XIII, A, 1). He essayed almost every
literary form. His poetry (XIII, B and D, 3) is important; most of it is published in his *Parnaso español*

(1648). His drama is unimportant. His prose is most important. The *Buscón* and *Sueños*, his two greatest works, belong chiefly to the picaresque type, and are satiric, burlesque, and *conceptista* (see XIII, D). Quevedo is Spain's greatest wit and satirist.

(a) *Vida del buscón, llamado don Pablos de Segovia* (1626; probably composed many years earlier). With cynical satire and caricature of types, this work is true to the form of the picaresque novel. It contains some fine scenes from a student boarding house.

(b) *Sueños* (1627). Was one of the most widely read and imitated books in Europe. It is a series of five visions (written in 1606, 1607, 1608, 1610, 1621– 1622) of the author visiting Hell. It does not follow strictly the picaresque formula. It is the boldest, bitterest, funniest social satire of the Golden Age.

(c) Didactic prose. *Política de Dios* (first part 1617– 1626; second part 1635–1655); *Marco Bruto* (1631– 1644). Various political, moral, and religious works.

8. Alonso Jerónimo de Salas Barbadillo (1581–1635). Lived by his pen and wrote much: verse, plays, and chiefly novels. Picaresque elements run all through his works.

*La hija de Celestina, o*

(a) *La ingeniosa Elena* (1612). Tricks and satirizes her lovers. The influence of this work in France was considerable: Scarron's *Hypocrite* (1654) and Molière's *Tartuffe* (1664). This is his best picaresque novel.

(b) *El sutil cordobés, Pedro de Urdemalas* (1620). Describes a literary academy, which opens the way for much extraneous material.

(c) *Don Diego de noche* (1623). Introduces the innovation of telling the story in the form of letters.

9. Alonso de Castillo Solórzano (1584–1647?). Like Salas Barbadillo, he wrote for money, much drama and verse but chiefly novels, with picaresque elements dominant. He wrote a series of three picaresque novels: *La niña de los embustes, Teresa del Manzanares* (1632), *Las aventuras del bachiller Trapaza* (1637), and *La garduña*

*de Sevilla y anzuelo de bolsas* (1642), adventures of the
daughter of Trapaza and Teresa.

10. Luis Vélez de Guevara y Dueñas (1579–1644). Was
well known as a dramatist in his day, but he is better
known today for his picaresque novel, *El diablo cojuelo*
(1641). A demon raises the roofs of homes so we can
see the life inside. This was a new idea and became very
popular. Famous is the French adaptation by Lesage
in *Le diable boiteux* (1707).

Rom-Nav., ch. 20, ch. 23, pp. 252–253, 255–256, 365;
Northup, pp. 169–190, 304–306; Mer-Mor., pp. 201–206,
274–278, 304–306, 314–322, 393–399; F. W. Chandler:
*Romances of roguery* (New York 1899); F. W. Chandler:
*Literature of roguery* (Boston 1907); F. DeHaan: *Outline
of the history of the novela picaresca in Spain* (New York
1903).

C. MIGUEL DE CERVANTES SAAVEDRA (1547–1616). Born in
Alcalá de Henares, of a Cordovan family, son of a poor
physician. He had little formal education, but read widely
(Classics in translation, Italian and Spanish authors) and
was schooled by experience. A soldier in Italy, his left
hand was crippled in the battle of Lepanto (1571). Re-
turning to Spain with letters of high recommendation, he
was captured (1575) and spent five eventful years in Algiers
as a slave. He was ransomed in 1580. The bulk of his
literary activity was late in life: from *Galatea* (1585; see
XV, A, 3) to *Persiles y Sigismunda* (1617; see XV, E, 1).
As a government official he had difficulty with his accounts,
and was imprisoned (1597). The publication of the first
part of *Don Quijote* in 1605 brought him late but instant
fame. He died of dropsy. The best literary interpre-
tation of him is seen through *Don Quijote.* He wrote
many lyrics and occasional verses, yet he realized his lack
of poetic genius. His *Viaje del Parnaso* (1614), an uncritical
survey of contemporary poets, imitated the Italian Cesare
Caporali's *Viaggio di Parnaso* (1582). For his drama see
XIV, B. Cervantes is called by many the world's greatest
novelist.

1. *El ingenioso hidalgo don Quijote de la Mancha* (first part
1605; second part 1615). The first part averaged one
edition a year for the first ten years. Its success tempted

<u>Vida y hechos de Estebanillo</u>
<u>González</u> (1646) — autobiographical
work, author unknown. Last
picaresque novel?

Alonso Fernández de Avellaneda (may be a pen name) to publish a spurious and inferior second part (1614). This spurred on Cervantes to finish his second part. He set out with the purpose of satirizing the imaginative excesses and other evils of chivalric novels; and at the same time, of giving a synthesis of all the best these novels had to offer. Idealism and realism are symbolized in Don Quijote and Sancho Panza. The author's viewpoint broadened as his work progressed. His philosophic maturity is manifest especially in the second part. Absolute originality, universality, broad humanity, sympathy, and humor make this work a classic. It gives a varied picture of 16th century society, with a rich variety of episodes interspersed. The style is adapted to the character and tone of the episode. Many consider this the world's greatest novel.

2. *Novelas ejemplares* (1613). Would have given Cervantes' name first rank in this section, even without *Don Quijote*. Cervantes called them " exemplary," like exempla (V, A), with decency of morals, to dissociate them from the savor of lack of morality typical of the Italian *novelle*. He claimed to be the first to write original *novelas* in Spanish. His *Novelas ejemplares* (written probably during 1600–1610) number twelve (thirteen with the *Tía fingida*), and fall into three general groups.

   (a) Those in which realistic and picaresque elements predominate. *Rinconete y Cortadillo* (XV, B, 6) is the best. *El celoso extremeño* tells of an old man, his young wife, and her gallant lover. In *La ilustre fregona* a kitchen-maid of good family marries an adventurous student. *El casamiento engañoso* was written as an introduction to the *Coloquio de los perros*. These form Cervantes' best and most original contribution to the *novela ejemplar*.

   (b) Philosophic dialogues. *El licenciado vidriera* (see XXXI, A, 3) contains the wise sayings of a man who thought he was made of glass. *El coloquio de los perros* (XV, B, 6) contains wise observations by a dog.

   (c) Those based on Italian models or resembling Italian patterns. The interest in these lies chiefly in plot

and episode. *La gitanilla* is a romance of gypsy life; *El amante liberal* describes captives' woes in Argel; *La española inglesa* portrays the English court; *Las dos doncellas*, disguised as men, pursue their lovers, and each gets her man; *La fuerza de la sangre* crowns abduction with marriage; *La señora Cornelia* suffers the woes of a secret marriage.

(d) *La tía fingida*. Not included in the *Novelas ejemplares*. It was published first by Agustín García Arrieta in his *Espíritu de Cervantes* (1814), and attributed to Cervantes by him, but the authorship is doubtful.

Rom-Nav., ch. 21;  Northup, ch. 15;  Mer-Mor., pp. 295–313.

D. MOORISH.  Literary fancy exploited the brilliantly contrasting Christian and Moorish society in southern Spain, chiefly in the late 16th century.  Here begins the exotic Oriental strain, so popular with the Romanticists in the early 19th century.

1. *El Abencerraje (y la hermosa Jarifa)*. This short, anonymous tale apparently grew up traditionally in the early 16th century.  The Moor, Abindarráez, of Granada, is captured (about 1485) on the way to his wedding, by the Spaniard, Narváez;  promises to return in three days after his wedding;  keeps his word, and is freed. The story is preserved in three different forms: (1) included by Antonio de Villegas in his *Inventario* (1565); (2) a more rhetorical form inserted in the fourth book of Montemayor's *Diana* (1561; XV, A, 1) by an unknown hand; (3) still a different form in an extract of a chronicle of Fernando de Antequera (probably mid-16th century).  Narváez is the ideal Renascence gentleman — brave, loyal, courteous, above all magnanimous.  The *Abencerraje* is the best of this type, and the model for all later novels of the type.

2. Ginés Pérez de Hita (1544?–1619?).  Wrote an *Historia de los bandos de los Zegríes y Abencerrajes*, popularly called *Guerras civiles de Granada* (first part 1595, second part 1604).  This hybrid history-novel is founded on historic fact, with fictitious characters and fantastic adventures added.  The first part, more fictitious, is on the fall of Granada (1492).  The second part, more

Algiers

4. López *El remedio* en la desdicha

historic, is on the Morisco rebellion of 1568–1571 in Granada (see XVII, A, 1, *c*).  The work abounds in vivid local color of Granada, with border ballads interspersed.  It was influential abroad: in France, Mlle de Scudéry, *Almahide* (1660); Mme de la Fayette, *Zaïde* (1670); Chateaubriand, *Aventures du dernier Abencérage* (1826); and in America, Washington Irving, *Chronicle of the conquest of Granada* (1829).

Rom-Nav., pp. 211–214; Northup, pp. 157–159; Mer-Mor., pp. 201, 294–295.

E. MILESIAN.  A modern continuation of a typical pattern of late Greek fiction; romantic adventures are suggested by the uncertainties of travel on the eastern Mediterranean in early times: pirates, shipwrecks, loved ones separated and reunited by chance (an overworked motive in this type).  The *Libro de Apolonio* (II, B, 2, *a*) is the first Spanish example of this type.  Many ancient works of the kind circulated in Renascence prose, such as *Teágenes y Cariclea*, by Heliodorus, a Greek writer from Syria of the 3rd century.  This work was widely translated and imitated in 16th century Spanish.

*[margin annotation: Byzantine Romances]*

Cervantes' *Persiles y Sigismunda* (1617).  From fantastic regions of ice and snow, the heroes come to France, Spain, and finally Rome.  This work is polished in style, complex in plot, with many autobiographic allusions.  It is as fantastic as the novels of chivalry.  The last part is more realistic and readable.  It gives us one example, from a noble pen, of this minor type.

Rom-Nav., pp. 268–270; Northup, pp. 159–160; Mer-Mor., pp. 302–304.

**XVI. Mysticism.**  Means the direct, conscious union of the soul with God; and can be accomplished in this life.  The Mystic way is composed of three stages: (1) purgative, excluding all external forces, forgetting the outside world and concentrating within, practiced with vocal prayer; (2) illuminative, introversion (*recogimiento*) and prayer of quietude, the will only being active and concentrated on forgetting oneself; (3) unitive, complete fusion (not annihilation) of the soul with God (spiritual marriage), the Supreme Power being active while the soul and its faculties are passive except in a calm effort for

Mateo Alemán (1547-1614?) included a longish Moorish tale: "Historia de Ozmín y Daraja" in Guzmán de Alfarache (1599) [chap. 8, Book I, Part I]

← Byzantine Romance
    [Short Stories]

María de Zayas Sotomayor (1590-1668?)
    Novelas ejemplares y amorosas (1637)
    Parte segunda del sarao y
        entretenimiento honestos (1647)
    — Scarron & Molière got some
        ideas from her

Juan de Timoneda (    -1583), friend
of Lope de Rueda, wrote plays and El
patrañuelo, 22 tales largely from
the Italian or earlier collections.

unity. Mystics practiced asceticism (bodily self-mortification). Mysticism is a recorded experience rather than a philosophy, open to everyone, though few attain it. Aware of the danger of too much introspection, the Mystics balanced their lives with periods of social activity. Their works contain delicate psychological analyses, and are concerned with practical morality. The Mystics were greatly interested in reform within the Church. They produced the finest lyrics and some of the most lucid prose of the Golden Age.

A. SAN JUAN DE LA CRUZ (Juan de Yepes y Álvarez) (1542–1591). Gives the best description of the higher stages, particularly in his poems, *Cántico espiritual entre el alma y el esposo*, *Noche oscura del alma*, and *Llama de amor viva* (the first was not published until 1627, the second and third in 1618). He accompanies these poems with long prose commentaries. He describes best the " dark night of the senses" which comes between the first and second stages, and the " dark night of the soul" which comes between the second and third stages. He used the *lira* (a combination of seven and eleven-syllable lines) most effectively. Solomon's *Song of Songs* (a book of the Old Testament) inspired him to describe the Mystic union in terms of human passions. He is the greatest of the Mystics.

B. SANTA TERESA DE JESÚS (Teresa Sánchez de Cepeda y Ahumada) (1515–1582). Her life is revealed to us in more than 400 letters (1561–1582); in her *Libro de las fundaciones* (1573), of her organizing activity; and in her autobiography, *Libro de su vida* (1562–1565). Her best work is in prose; her verse is mediocre. Her best Mystic work is *El castillo interior* or *Las moradas* (1588), which describes the whole Mystic process as she experienced it. She knew no literary style but wrote as she would speak. Her Mystic flame is given further expression in her *Camino de perfección* (1585) and *Conceptos del amor de Dios o Cantares* (1611). She described the Mystic way in a most tangible, material form.

C. LUIS DE GRANADA (Luis Sarria) (1504–1588). Won fame as a preacher; was chosen Dominican Provincial of Portugal (1556); wrote much in Latin, Spanish, and Portuguese. He is more a theologian than an experienced Mystic.

1. *Guía de pecadores* (1556). Shows how to attain to a virtuous life. This is his most popular work.

2. *Introducción del símbolo de la fe* (1583). An encyclopedic synthesis of the science of Christianity, and an
   apologetic history of Catholicism, showing the layman
   how to rise by faith and reason through the mysteries
   of the Church. He has an oratorical, Ciceronian style,
   and colorful imagery. He popularized the Church
   Fathers (quoted them extensively).
3. *Libro de la oración y meditación* (1554). A manual of
   ascetic practices, prayer, and contemplation.

D. LUIS PONCE DE LEÓN (1527–1591). A Humanist who
   defended Spanish. His works show both Hebraic and
   Classic influence. He was a theology professor at Salamanca. He renounced a life of pleasure, which family
   income could afford, and became an Augustinian monk.
   He translated Solomon's *Song of Songs*, which for him
   expressed the essence of Mysticism, directly from Hebrew
   into Spanish (about 1561), was accused by jealous colleagues
   of lack of respect for the Vulgate (official Latin version of
   the Bible in the Catholic Church, originally made by St.
   Jerome in the 4th century), and of being of Jewish descent,
   and was imprisoned (1572) by the Inquisition, but was re-
   leased (1576), and returned to teach at Salamanca. He was
   always fearlessly outspoken. He progressed far along the
   Mystic way, but regretted that he never attained union in
   this life. Luis de León is called by some Spain's greatest
   lyric poet (XIII, A, 1). He is also a master of clear and precise prose.

   see p. 48

   1. *De los nombres de Cristo* (1583). Seeks to understand
      Christ through a study of his names (Shepherd, Son of
      God, King, Jesus, the Beloved, etc.), discussed in a Pla-
      tonic dialogue of three monks. He includes fine descrip-
      tions of nature, sees God's works in nature, and makes
      excellent use of nature similes in New Testament style.
      This is his best-known work.
   2. *La perfecta casada* (1583). Describes the model house-
      wife: early to bed and early to rise . . . ; silence is
      golden; on the use of cosmetics; etc.

      Rom-Nav., ch. 14, ch. 17; Northup, ch. 10; Mer-Mor.,
      pp. 263–273.

XVII. **Didactic literature.** Sebastián de Covarruvias Orozco's

*Tesoro de la lengua castellana o española* (1611, revised 1674–1673) is the best dictionary produced in the Golden Age.

Mer-Mor., pp. 273–274, 281–288.

A. HISTORY.

1. National.

(a) Juan de Mariana (1536–1624). This Jesuit and independent thinker, wishing to inform Europe of Spain's great past, wrote his *Historia de España* first in Latin (twenty books in 1592, increased finally to thirty in 1605), then he translated it into Spanish for the local public (1601). Like his model, the Roman historian Livy (59–17 B.C.), he enlivened his work with colorful legends, making it a work of art. It covers from earliest times to Carlos V (ruled 1516–1556). Mariana is probably Spain's best-known historian.

(b) Prudencio de Sandoval (1551?–1620). His *Historia de la vida y hechos del emperador Carlos V* (1604–1606) supplements Mariana's work.

(c) Diego Hurtado de Mendoza (1503–1575). His *Guerra de Granada* (not published until 1627) is on the Morisco rebellion of 1568–1571 (see XV, D, 2). The author lived banished in Granada during this time. His style is concise, his viewpoint impartial. He is also noted for his poetry (1610).

Rom-Nav., pp. 173–177; Northup, pp. 202–204; Mer-Mor., pp. 256–262, 390–393.

2. AMERICAN.

(a) El Inca, Garcilaso de la Vega (1540?–1615). Was the son of a cousin of the poet Garcilaso (VIII, A, 2) and an Inca princess. He wrote after retiring from military service, and was the first South American author of note in Spanish literature. His *Florida del Inca* (1605) deals with the adventures of Hernando de Soto (1496?–1542), discoverer of the Mississippi. He also wrote *Comentarios reales que tratan del origen de los Incas* (1609–1617).

(b) Antonio de Solís y Rivadeneyra (1610–1686). Appointed chronicler of the Indies in 1665. His great

work was his *Historia de la conquista de Méjico* (1684), which covers only the three years up to the taking of the capital (1519–1521). He made this a work of art, with fine sketches of scenes and characters. See XII, A, 2, *b*. As a disciple of Calderón he wrote several dramas.

Rom-Nav., pp. 173–174, 412–413; Northup, pp. 207–208; Mer-Mor., pp. 259–260, 392.

B. PROVERBS. Active collection continued. See VI, C. Gonzalo Correas' (died 1631) *Vocabulario de refranes* is one of the finest in Spanish; however, it lay in manuscript until 1906. The Frenchman, César Oudin, who was a well-known Spanish teacher, produced a collection of *Refranes o proverbios españoles traducidos en lengua francesa* (1605). Juan Sorapán de Rieros wrote a *Medicina española contenida en proverbios vulgares de nuestra lengua* (1616–1615).

Northup, p. 132; Mer-Mor., pp. 191–192, 287.

C. BALTASAR GRACIÁN Y MORALES (1601–1658). An Aragonese Jesuit, a great philosopher, and the greatest prose writer of the Gongoristic group. His style is concise and highly polished but obscure.

*El criticón.* A philosophic novel, published in three parts: youth (1651), maturity (1653), old age (1657). It contains much allegory. Critilo, a civilized man of judgment and experience, brings Andrenio, a man of nature, into contact with civilization. The author's pessimistic philosophic observations favor a primitive state. This is his masterpiece.

Rom-Nav., pp. 405–412; Northup, pp. 303–304; Mer-Mor., pp. 279–281; A. F. G. Bell: *Baltasar Gracián* (Oxford 1921).

# EIGHTEENTH CENTURY

Mer-Mor., pp. 365–370, 403–411; Chapman, chs. 31–38.

**XVIII. Didactic literature.** The most important chapter in Neoclassic 18th century literature, many of whose contributions to erudition have not yet been rendered obsolete. The Na-

18th cent., lowest ebb of Sp. lit.

Neo - Classicism

Aftermath of Renascence

This century dominated by didacticism.

The Spaniards very slavishly tried to imitate the classics.

{ Fable - literature revived
  epic poetry

tional Library was founded in 1712. Much text and periodical publication was begun.

A. (REAL) ACADEMIA ESPAÑOLA. Founded in 1714.

    1. *Diccionario de la lengua castellana*, popularly called *Diccionario de autoridades*, was first published in six volumes (1726-1739). All subsequent editions, down to the 15th in 1925, have been in one volume. A revision of the first edition in many volumes is now beginning publication. The *Diccionario de autoridades* is supplemented, for scientific terms, by Esteban de Terreros y Pando's *Diccionario castellano con las voces de ciencias y artes* (1786-1793).

    2. The Academy's *Gramática* first appeared in 1771; there have been many editions since. This work is far below the Academy's dictionary in quality.

B. ACADEMIA DE LA HISTORIA. Founded in 1738. History becomes less artistic, but is placed on a more accurate and scientific basis, as in Juan Ferreras' *Sinopsis histórica cronológica de España* (1700-1716). One of the greatest monuments of the period is Enrique Flórez's *España sagrada* in 52 volumes published from 1747 to 1918. Florez wrote the first 29 volumes, and others continued the work. It is a history of the Church in Spain.

C. BENITO JERÓNIMO FEIJÓO Y MONTENEGRO (1676-1764). A Benedictine, from Galicia, and a professor of philosophy and theology at Oviedo. His *Teatro crítico universal* (1726-1739) in eight volumes plus one of corrections and supplements (1741) was complemented by his *Cartas eruditas y curiosas* in five volumes (1742-1760). These fourteen volumes form a general encyclopedia, with essays on literature, language, superstitions, philosophy, etc. He attacks both impenetrable *españolismo* (see XXVII) and those who adopt foreign ideas to the extreme. He catalogues current ideas, opinions, and errors; and tries to clear knowledge of prejudice and superstition. He attacks Gongorism (XIII, D). He believes in literary rules, but not when they hamper real artistic genius.

D. IGNACIO LUZÁN CLARAMUNT DE SUELVES Y GURREA (1702-1754). This cosmopolitan Aragonese, educated in Italy, was secretary to the Spanish embassy in Paris, and spoke German. He saw that the realistic exuberance of

el español —written— standard Spanish

el castellano —properly— the dialect of Castile

Feijóo wanted to combat superstition

Luzán was the greatest literary critic of the 18$^{th}$ cent.

the Renascence had been smothered by Gongorism, and now was the time to revive and regulate Spanish poetry to a rational, sensible medium; hence his *Poética* (1737; revised, incorporating the deceased author's manuscript corrections and additions, 1789). The first volume deals with poetry in general; the second with the drama and the epic. His chief sources are Italian Renascence interpreters of the Greek philosopher Aristotle (384–322 B.C.). He advocates: observance of the three unities and decorum; imitating nature; verisimilitude; *utile dulci* (" useful-sweet"); that is, literature with a practical, useful or didactic purpose, and at the same time beautiful, pleasant and entertaining); using blank verse, also ballad meter. The *auto sacramental* (see XIV, H, 3) is condemned; the Christian marvelous is recommended instead of Classic mythology; and he does see good in Lope de Vega and Calderón (XIV, C and H). Luzán's *Poética* is probably the best-known Spanish treatise on the art of poetry.

Rom-Nav., ch. 30, p. 444; Northup, pp. 314–318; Mer-Mor., pp. 412–416, 444–450.

**XIX. Fable.** In an age of didacticism, instructive poetry was bound to bloom, and the fable, or versified apologue or moral short story, often with animal characters, flowered in the late 18th century, following the tradition of that legendary Greek fable writer Æsop (620–560 B.C.), whose Fables had long been known in Spain (first known edition, 1489), and were known in contemporary publication (Pedro Simón Abril's Spanish edition of 1761).

A. Tomás de Iriarte y Oropesa (1750–1791).

1. *Fábulas literarias* (1782). Iriarte invented his own fables, which give rules for good writing and attack prominent contemporary literary figures. His satire has moderation and good taste. His verse shows metrical variety. This is the classic of Spanish fable literature.
2. *La música* (1779). An elegant Neoclassic didactic poem.
3. Two brilliant comedies of manners: *La señorita malcriada* (1788). *El señorito mimado* (1788).

B. Félix María Samaniego (1745–1801). This Basque gentleman wrote especially for seminary pupils his *Fábulas morales* (first part 1781, second part 1784). It has many

Fable: short story to illustrate a moral point, usually with animal characters — usually in verse.

original fables, although some are from the earlier fabulists (Classics).

Rom-Nav., pp. 452–455; Northup, pp. 320–321, 326; Mer-Mor., pp. 434–435.

**XX. Lyric poetry.** In this didactic age, prose flourished more than poetry, which lacked originality and sought authority in poetic traditions and Italian verse. Most of this group, known as the Salamancan school, were active in the late 18th century.

A. JOSÉ CADALSO Y VÁZQUEZ DE ANDRADE (1741–1782). Traveled widely through Europe, and was a foreign imitator. His anacreontics (lyrics like those of Anacreon, Greek poet, about 500 B.C., who sang of wine and women, in seven-syllable verses) and elegies (songs of lamentation, especially for the dead) enjoyed contemporary favor. He also wrote a Classic tragedy, *Sancho García* (1771), and prose *Cartas marruecas* (1793, but written in 1768), following a plan similar to that in Montesquieu's French *Lettres persanes* (1721), in which a fictitious Moor finds much to criticize in Spanish society. His prose *Noches lúgubres* (1798), suggested by Edward Young's English *Night Thoughts* (1742–1745), was inspired by his romantic love for the actress, María Ignacia Ibáñez, and her death. A founder and leader of the Salamancan group, Cadalso influenced later members (Jovellanos and Meléndez Valdés). He wrote mostly Classicism and lived Romanticism.

B. GASPAR MELCHOR DE JOVELLANOS (1744–1811). A prominent statesman of advanced ideas, who championed Spain's cause against France, and was a vehement defender of nationalism. His economic report on reforms in agricultural laws, *Informe sobre la ley agraria* (1795), is a prose masterpiece. Even his poetry is like prose. He excelled in didactic and satiric verse, usually with a moral or philosophic aim. He is a Classicist, with reason dominating emotion. Besides poetry, he wrote *El delincuente honrado* (1774), a melodramatic play in prose; and *Pelayo* (1814, written as *Munuza* in 1769), a tragedy. His basic contribution was a life of action, powerfully expressed in his writings.

C. JUAN MELÉNDEZ VALDÉS (1754–1817). A Salamanca professor and politician. He wrote anacreontics and eclogues, which include his best work, as *Batilo* (1780). *La gloria de*

Cadalso - forerunner of Romanticism

*las artes* (1781) is a didactic ode; later he aspired to the philosophic and political ode. At the end of the century he followed the fashion of English poetry: Young's *Night Thoughts* and Pope's *Essay on Man* (1732–1734). He also wrote a play, *Las bodas de Camacho* (1784). Wavering external sweetness characterizes his poetry as well as his political career. He attained the most polished form of any of the Neoclassic poets.

D. MANUEL JOSÉ QUINTANA (1772–1857). Most of his active period lies in the early 19th century, but he belongs to this group. He lived through the Romantic period, but was unaffected by it. Like Jovellanos, he was a poet, patriot, philosopher, and politician, intensely national. He wrote the first draft of his poems in prose, and his poems show this.

1. He is at his best in the Classic ode, inspired by patriotism and liberalism: *Al armamento de las provincias españolas contra los franceses* (1808); *A España después de la revolución de marzo* (1808); *A la paz entre España y Francia en 1795* (1797). These are Classic in form, fiery in emotion.

2. As a literary critic he wrote *Las reglas del drama* (1791), based on the *Art poétique* of the French writer Boileau (1674).

3. Two tragedies: *El duque de Viseo* (1801); *Pelayo* (1805). The latter is better than the dramatic treatment of the same theme by Nicolás Fernández de Moratín and Jovellanos.

4. His best prose work is his *Vidas de los españoles célebres* (1807–1833), biographies of the Cid, Guzmán el Bueno, Roger de Lauria, el Príncipe de Viana, Gonzalo de Córdoba, Vasco Núñez de Balboa, Pizarro, Álvaro de Luna, and Bartolomé de las Casas.

Rom-Nav., pp. 440–443, 448–452, 455–463; Northup, pp. 319–320, 321–323; Mer-Mor., pp. 413–414, 426–434, 435–439.

**XXI. Drama.** The chief arena for struggles between the Neoclassicists and the Nationalists. Dramatic rules were established by Luzán (XVIII, D) in the early 18th century. The bulk of the dramas were published in the late 18th century. Luzán's principles were sustained by the influential *Academia del buen gusto*, which held literary *tertulias* in the house of the

countess of Lemos during 1749–1751. Agustín de Montiano y Luyando (1697–1764), a leader of this academy, hotly denounced Cervantes and Lope de Vega, and advocated Neoclassic rules and French models in two *Discursos sobre las tragedias españolas* (1750 and 1753), accompanied by two stiff tragedies as examples: *Virginia* (1750) and *Ataulfo* (1753), observing the three unities and even a fourth, unity of character (a character must portray one outstanding trait). Nicolás Fernández de Moratín's (1737–1780, father of Leandro — XXI, B) *Hormesinda* (1770) ran only six nights; two other tragedies by him, *Lucrecia* (1763) and *Guzmán el Bueno* (1777), were never produced. Moratín began the *Tertulia de la fonda de San Sebastián*, which sustained the tradition of the *Academia del buen gusto*. The count of Aranda, minister of Carlos III (ruled 1759–1788), was a vigorous protector of the *galicistas*. Vicente Antonio García de la Huerta's (1734–1787) *Raquel* (1778), on the same theme as Lope de Vega's *Judía de Toledo* (1617), scored greater success. All Neoclassic tragedies are insipid. Iriarte's *Señorito mimado* (XIX, A, 3) was a real success as a Neoclassic comedy.

A. RAMÓN FRANCISCO DE LA CRUZ CANO Y OLMEDILLA (1731–1794). This prolific Madrilenian wrote over 500 plays; some tragedies, but mostly *sainetes* (one-act, jocose dramatic sketches, an amplification of the *entremés*, in ballad meter, frequently of customs and satire of folktypes, often presented at the conclusion of a longer drama), which were popular among all classes. He published his collected dramas or *Teatro* (1786–1791). His *sainetes*, such as *Las castañeras picadas*, *La casa de Tócame-Roque*, *El Prado por la noche*, *La Plaza Mayor por Navidad*, and *El fandango del candil*, accurately and smilingly portray contemporary life. His lower class types speak in dialect. His rule was "Yo escribo y la verdad me dicta." Even when he borrowed from the Italian dramatist Goldoni (1707–1793), or the French, Molière (1622–1673) and Racine (1639–1699), or Shakespeare (1564–1616), the result was very Spanish. Neoclassic criticism prevailed little against his return to colorful, realistic, native tradition, portrayed in his *sainetes*, which sustain his name high in the drama.

B. LEANDRO FERNÁNDEZ DE MORATÍN (1760–1828). Born in Madrid, he held various diplomatic posts, traveled widely, and learned several languages. *La derrota de los*

← García de la Huerta in 1785 published Theatro Hespañol with 16 volumes of old "comedias," from which he omitted Lope, Tirso, Alarcón, Vélez de Guevara, Guillén de Castro, etc.

*pedantes* (1789) is a keen literary satire in prose. His
*Orígenes del teatro español* (not published till 1830, incomplete) is a treatise on the early Spanish drama. He is an
excellent portrayer of affairs of the heart. Like Ramón de
la Cruz, he translated Shakespeare's *Hamlet* (written
shortly after 1600) in 1798. He wrote five original plays:
*El viejo y la niña* (1790) in verse; *La comedia nueva, o El
café* (1792) in prose; *El barón* (1803) in verse; *La mojigata*
(1804) in verse; *El sí de las niñas* (1806) in prose. Some of
these were written long before they were produced. Moratín blended common-sense proportion and Neoclassic pre-
cepts with native tradition. He respected the Golden Age
drama. His plays are simple in basic plot, richly imaginative
in detail, perfect and simple in expression, and are characterized by sameness in themes and types in middle-class
comedy. *El sí de las niñas* advances the modern thesis that
parents should not arrange marriage without the consent
of the lovers concerned, follows the traditional Spanish
three-act division instead of the Classic five, and portrays
native types, using language true to character. Moratín
represents the peak of 18th century comedy.

Rom-Nav., ch. 31; Northup, pp. 325–331; Mer-Mor.,
pp. 416–425.

**XXII. Novel.** The least active type in this century, produced
only one masterpiece: *Fray Gerundio.*

A. DIEGO DE TORRES Y VILLARROEL (1693–1770). Lived
the life of a *pícaro*, which he portrays in novelistic fashion
in his best work, his *Vida* (1743–1758). He was a poet,
bullfighter, quack doctor, soothsayer, mathematics professor at Salamanca, beggar, etc. He makes a frank state-
ment of conditions in contemporary society. He gained
much money and popularity by the publication of long
series of *Pronósticos* and *Almanaques* under the pen name
of *El gran Piscator de Salamanca.* He imitated his favorite
author, Quevedo (XV, B, 7), in his *Sueños morales, visiones
y visitas de Torres con don Francisco de Quevedo por Madrid*
(1743). He published a volume of plays, *Juguetes de
Talía* (1738).

B. JOSÉ FRANCISCO DE ISLA Y ROJO (1703–1781). A Jesuit.

1. *Historia del famoso predicador Fray Gerundio de Cam-
pazas, alias Zotes.* The best novel of the century. The

first volume (1758) sold rapidly, but was censored, and
the second volume did not appear until 1768. This is a
comic, satiric parody of contemporary pulpit bombast.
His own *Sermones* (1792–1793) show him to be a master
of his subject.

2. He translated from the French Lesage's *Gil Blas* (1715–
1735) in 1787–1788, a belated picaresque novel which
Lesage had modeled on earlier Spanish examples of the
type see XV, B, 5). So excellent and purely Spanish is
Isla's rendering that, together with his false claim
that he was " restoring " the work to its original tongue,
many believed it really was originally Spanish.

3. *Triunfo del amor, y de la lealtad. Día grande de Navarra*
(1746). An ironic prose account of the celebration at
Pamplona on the accession of Fernando VI (in 1746).
It created a stir when its satiric force was realized.

4. *Cartas familiares* (1789–1794). Form the best epistolary
literature of the age.

Rom-Nav., pp. 439–440, 445–446; Northup, pp. 331–334;
Mer-Mor., pp. 450–452.

# NINETEENTH CENTURY

Rom-Nav., ch. 34; Mer-Mor., pp. 455–463, 501–508; Chapman, ch. 39.

## XXIII. Poetry.

A. SEVILLIAN SCHOOL. Represents a transition period at the
end of the 18th century and about the first quarter of the
19th century, up to Romanticism. A group of cultured
educators, notably Alberto Lista, formed the *Academia de
letras humanas* (in 1793) to instruct the public in good
taste. They followed many Neoclassic ideas. They lacked
originality and inspiration; spontaneity was smothered by
laborious, pedantic bombast. They were the Fray Ge-
rundios (see XXII, B, 1) of poetry. They admitted Biblical
themes, which was a departure from Classic precept.

Alberto Lista y Aragón (1775–1848). Was the school-
master of Espronceda (XXIII, B, 1) and Ventura de la
Vega (1807–1865). His *Imperio de la estupidez* (1798) is

an imitation of Alexander Pope's *Dunciad* (1728).
His *Poesías* were published in 1822 and 1837. He
was a literary critic. He is a sufficient example of this
school.

Rom-Nav., pp. 508–509; Northup, pp. 323–324; Mer-Mor.,
pp. 439–443.

B. ROMANTIC. As a particular movement Romanticism had
a short, intense life in Spain, mostly in poetry and drama,
chiefly in the 1830's. It was a reaction against Neoclassicism,
of feeling against form, of Christianity (Catholicism)
against Paganism (Classic mythology). Interest was
centered on nature, folklore, local color, and the national
past (Middle and Golden Ages); and there was a general
tone of pessimism. The existence of most of these traits
to a certain degree previously in Spain made the reaction
less violent; for many Spaniards Romanticism was, in
great part, merely a return to native tradition. This movement prompted the publication of many ballad collections,
the most notable of which is that of Agustín Durán in
1828–1832; and of older monuments of Spanish poetry;
indeed, as early as 1779 Tomás Antonio Sánchez published
his *Colección de poesías castellanas anteriores al siglo XV*,
which included the *Poema de Mío Cid* (II, A, 1, *g*), which
was earlier than the publication by Germany of her great
medieval epic, the *Nibelungenlied*, or by France of hers,
the *Chanson de Roland*. Liberals were forced to leave Spain
under Fernando VII (ruled 1814–1833), going chiefly to
London and Paris. Abroad these *emigrados* absorbed
Romanticism, and gave great impetus to the movement
when they returned in 1833, after Fernando VII's death.
Lyric poetry was the best form for unrestrained expression
of emotion.

1. José de Espronceda y Delgado (1808–1842). A born
rebel and radical. Influences upon him were many and
varied. His collected *Poesías* (1840) express many
themes and moods: *Canción del pirata*, *El mendigo*,
*El verdugo*, *A la noche*, *A la patria*. His *Estudiante de
Salamanca* is the poetic legend of a Romantic Don Juan.
*El diablo mundo* (1841) is an unfinished philosophic poem
of disillusion: Adam, virtuous and innocent by nature,
is thrown against a cruel world; this is a confused, fan-

tastic medley, with brilliant flashes. Espronceda is the best example of a Spanish Romantic poet.

2. José Zorrilla. Most famed for his Romantic drama (XXIV, A, 5). But he is also in the first rank among Romantic lyric poets. At the age of twenty at Larra's burial (1837) he appeared, unknown, read his poetic tribute to Larra, and became famous overnight. Various collections of his verse were published in the late 1830's and early 1840's. *Ecos de las montañas* (1868); *El cantar del romero* (1883). He was a colorful improvisor, fluent and careless in expression. His work, like Lope de Vega's, should be viewed as a panoramic whole. He excelled in the verse *leyenda*.

   (a) *Cantos del trovador* (1840–1841). A richly imaginative portrayal of past ages.
   (b) *María* (1849). A poem, finished by the American, José Heriberto García de Quevedo (1819–1871), treating lyrically the life story of the Virgin.
   (c) *Granada* (1852, incomplete). A poem on the conquest of Granada by Fernando and Isabel in 1492, interspersed with various legends of the Alhambra.
   (d) *La leyenda del Cid* (1882). A poetic legend of this hero.

   Rom-Nav., pp. 483–495; Northup, pp. 343–348, 354–357, 358–360; Mer-Mor., pp. 465–473.

C. LATE 19TH CENTURY POETS. Display various tendencies: philosophy, skepticism, regionalism.

1. Gustavo Adolfo Domínguez Bécquer (1836–1870). Led a Bohemian life in Madrid; suffered disease and poverty; and died at thirty-four. Most of his excellent prose legends and *Desde mi celda, cartas literarias* were published first in the periodical *El contemporáneo* (1860–1864). Also at that time he composed his *Rimas* (1860–1861), about eighty short lyrics, through which runs a drama of love, sung in sorrowful and intimate tones; these constitute his best work. His collected works were published first in 1871. His delicate sentiment thrived best in solitude and amid ancient ruins. His tender longing for the ideal reminds us of the German Romanticists.

*Wehmut (Heine)*

2. Ramón María de las Mercedes de Campoamor y Campoosorio (1817–1901). A politician and physician of Asturias, who lived in comfortable circumstances. He wrote various short poems (1840, and many later editions) of philosophic and moral observations and sentimental memories. Most conflicting are the critical opinions about him. He claimed the invention of new poetic forms, notably *doloras* and *humoradas*.

   (*a*) *Doloras* (1846). Poems joining lightness with sentiment, concision with philosophic import; dramatizations of universal truths. They form his best work. His most popular *dolora* is *¡Quién supiera escribir!*

   (*b*) *Humoradas* (1886–1888). The gemlike essence of all forms of poetry, — poetic epigrams.

3. Gaspar Núñez de Arce (1832?–1903). Rose high in politics, and was interested in public welfare. He thought poetry should reflect the society from which it springs, and should touch the profoundest human emotions. He tried to reconcile faith and reason (see XXXI, B, 1). His tone is one of pessimistic *desengaño*. He used a great variety of verse forms. He is Romantic in thought, Neoclassic in expression.

   *Deplored political excesses of any kind*

   (*a*) *Gritos del combate* (1875). His best collection of lyrics.

   (*b*) *La pesca* (1884). A fisherman's love story in verse.

   (*c*) *La visión de Fray Martín* (1880). A lyricized epic sketch of Luther (1483–1546).

   (*d*) *El haz de leña* (1872). A drama about the tragic end of the son of Felipe II, Carlos, who, imprisoned by his father, died in 1568. Núñez de Arce tried drama early in his career, without much success.

   Rom-Nav., ch. 38; Northup, pp. 364–365, 403–409; Mer-Mor., pp. 509–519.

## XXIV. Drama.

A. ROMANTIC. Written chiefly in the 1830's. Herein we find the richest flowering of Romanticism.

   1. Francisco de Paula Martínez de la Rosa Berdejo Gómez y Arroyo (1787–1862). A prominent statesman from

Granada, who visited London in his youth, and spent most of the 1820's exiled in France. He opened the way for the Romantic drama. He was an eclectic experimenter, but always with moderation. His early works were Neoclassic, notably the tragedies *La viuda de Padilla* (1814) and *Edipo* (1829). His comedies continued the tradition of Moratín (XXI, B). In 1830 his *Apuntes sobre el drama histórico* shows a new but moderate shift. Also in 1830 he wrote the first two real Romantic dramas, in prose, with local color, disregarding unities, exotic, and with other Romantic traits:

(a) *Aben Humeya ou la Révolte des Maures sous Philippe II*. Produced in French in Paris (1830); text appeared in both French and Spanish. It is based on an incident in the war of the Alpujarran moriscos in 1568.

(b) *La conjuración de Venecia*. Written in exile in Paris, and staged in Madrid in 1834. It pictures passionate love and political intrigue in the Venice of 1310.

2. Ángel Pérez de Saavedra Ramírez de Madrid Remírez de Baquedano, Duke of Rivas (1791–1865). Of a rich Cordovan family, he fought against the French. His early poetry and drama (1810's and 1820's) are Neoclassic. In exile he visited England (1824) and Malta (1825–1830). His lyrics, *El desterrado* (1824) and *El faro de Malta* (1828), show Romantic traits. He went to France (1830), and fully adopted Romanticism. He returned to Spain (1834), and the last twenty-five years of his life were dedicated to politics and the administration of his estate. His greatest literary activity was in the 1830's.

(a) *Don Álvaro, o La fuerza del sino*. This drama was written first in France, in prose, in 1831, rewritten in mingled prose and verse, and staged in 1835. Don Álvaro is persecuted by Fate until he commits suicide. Even minor details are vividly elaborated, and minor characters are perfected. The opera *La forza del destino* (1862), by the Italian composer Verdi, is based on *Don Álvaro*, which is the typical and model Spanish Romantic drama.

(b) *El moro expósito* (1834). A Romantic epic legend,

Wrote a _Poética_ in verse (1827)
(Neo-classic ideas)

Before Romanticism, all dramas were
in verse —

Also in 1834: Mariano José de Larra,
_Macías_ [see p. 120]

planned in Malta in the 1820's. It is written in *romance heróico* (eleven-syllable verses with alternating assonance). It deals with the infantes of Lara and Mudarra (II, A, 1, *e*); Rivas' version is based rather on ballads. Córdova and Burgos are represented colorfully as centers of Moorish and Christian culture.

(*c*) *Romances históricos* (1841). These ballads treat subjects from all periods of Spanish history, and use the regular eight-syllable, assonating, *romance* form. They are an excellent artistic revival of the *romances históricos* (group 1 in Chapter IX). Rivas' training in painting shows up to good advantage in these colorful scenes. His preface is an important Romantic document.

3. Antonio García Gutiérrez (1813–1884). Traveled in Cuba, Mexico, France, and England. He wrote about seventy dramas through the mid-19th century, and some poetry: *Poesías* (1840) and *Luz y tinieblas* (1842).

(*a*) *El trovador* (1836). His most brilliant success in the Romantic drama. On it Verdi based his opera, *Il trovatore* (1853).

(*b*) Later dramas. Several are better than *El trovador*, but never became so popular: *Simón Bocanegra* (1843) and *Juan Lorenzo* (1865).

4. Juan Eugenio Hartzenbusch (1806–1880). The son of a German father and a Spanish mother, this self-taught cabinet maker and stenographer finally became director of the National Library in Madrid (1862). He was a zealous critic and editor of the Golden Age drama.

(*a*) *Los amantes de Teruel* (1836; first performed in January 1837). His first and best drama. It is a Romantic version of this famous legend (see XIV, F, 4).

(*b*) Comedies in the tradition of Moratín. *Los polvos de la madre Celestina* (1840); *La coja y el encogido* (1843).

(*c*) *Fábulas* (1848 and 1861). Show satire tempered with humor.

(*d*) *Ensayos poéticos* (1843); and fantastic prose tales.

5. José Zorrilla y Moral (1817–1893). See XXIII, B, 2 for his poetry. He tells of his life in *Recuerdos del tiempo viejo* (1880–1882). He led a long Bohemian life of poverty, traveled widely over Europe, married a lady old enough to be his mother, and fled from her to Mexico (1855–1866). He was a master improviser, careless in formal correctness. Abundant and varied are his dramas, and diverse are his sources, but he made his plays typically Spanish. He is essentially a lyric poet, even in his dramas. Brisk in action, lively in style, his plays often revive historic and legendary characters, with Romantic coloring. Zorrilla is the most popular Romantic dramatist.

   (a) *Don Juan Tenorio* (1844). See XIV, F, 1. Enjoyed the most sustained success of any Romantic drama. Tradition has made this play a regular part of the celebration of All Saints' Day (November 1st). Criticized for careless workmanship and inconsistencies, Zorrilla himself later condemned this play. But his blended fantastic, sensuous, religious, Romantic rendering of this popular story continues to be dear to the Spanish heart.

   (b) Other plays based on legends. Constitute the better part of his work. *El zapatero y el rey* (1840–1841) treats of Pedro el Cruel (ruled 1350–1369); *El puñal del godo* (1842) deals with Rodrigo (see II, A, 1, a).

   (c) Three-act verse *comedias de capa y espada* of the Golden Age type. *Cada cual con su razón* (1839); *Ganar perdiendo* (1839); *Más vale llegar a tiempo que rondar un año* (1845).

   Rom-Nav., pp. 474–483, 496–497; Northup, pp. 348–354, 357–358, 360–361; Mer-Mor., pp. 464–465, 474–481.

B. VARIOUS DRAMATIC CURRENTS OF THE CENTURY, mostly late 19th: the tradition of Moratín and the Golden Age drama; the thesis play; social satire; comedy; the historical play; the *género chico*.

   1. Manuel Bretón de los Herreros (1796–1873). His best period of literary activity was in the second quarter of the century. He wrote over 100 original plays, many translations and adaptations. He preferred to portray the middle class and women. His work is characterized

Most widely known of Romantic dramatists

Traidor, inconfeso y mártir (1849)
[Pastelero de Madrigal — Sebastião story]

by optimism, wit, humor, and indulgent satire (of Romanticism and foreign imitators). He wrote mostly in verse (*romance* and various forms), and gave popular expression to common emotions.

(*a*) *A la vejez viruelas* (1824). His first play; satirizes the aged lover.

(*b*) *Marcela, o ¿Cuál de los tres?* (1831). Portrays a young widow who wishes to live independently.

(*c*) *Muérete y verás* (1837). Shows a girl who, believing her lover dead, is quite ready to marry another.

(*d*) *La escuela del matrimonio* (1852). Considers three marriages, badly matched in age, social category, and education.

2. Manuel Tamayo y Baus (1829–1898). His dramatic production began with a translation at the age of eleven, and ceased at <u>forty-one</u>. Various currents are seen in his drama: Golden Age, Neoclassicism, Romanticism, foreign influence. A professional actor in his youth, he knew well how to handle technical problems.

*1870 elected Secretary of Spanish Academy*

(*a*) *Un drama nuevo* (1867). Portrays in simple prose Shakespeare and others of his troop. Betrayed by his wife, the clown Yorick plays a part that fits his real situation. This is his best play, and one of Spain's finest tragedies.

(*b*) *Virginia* (1853). Combines Romanticism with the Classic tragedy.

*typical of Tamayo y Baus*

(*c*) Historical dramas. *La locura de amor* (1855) deals with Juana la Loca (1479–1555), daughter of Fernando and Isabel, who was madly jealous of her husband.

*1867 Los hombres de bien [attacks hypocrisy]*

(*d*) Thesis plays. *La bola de nieve* (1856) attacks jealousy; *Lo positivo* (1862) attacks materialism; *Lances de honor* (1863) attacks dueling.

3. Adelardo López de Ayala y Herrera (1828–1879). Another thesis playwright. He knew well the Golden Age drama. *El tanto por ciento* (1861) and *Consuelo* (1878) attack those who crave wealth; *El nuevo don Juan* (1863) is against the male "vamp." He also wrote historical plays: *Un hombre de estado* (1851), etc., and *zarzuelas* (see XXIV, B, 6).

4. José Echegaray y Eizaguirre (1832–1916). A mathe-

was unaffected by Romanticism

Manuel Eduardo de Gorostiza
(1789-1851)
Contigo pan y cebolla (1833)

Actress, Teodora Lamadrid was
López de Ayala's mistress

*Elected to Academy of Science (1866); Academy de la lengua (1894)*

matics professor and politician [*minister of Treasury*] who turned to drama late in life. He began with *El libro talonario* (1874) at the age of forty-two, and ruled the Spanish stage in the last quarter of the century, writing more than sixty plays. He was a Nobel prize winner for literature in 1904.

(*a*) Thesis plays. Often unusual social problems are treated. *O locura o santidad* (1877) shows that honesty is not always the best policy; the strictly honest man is sometimes thought to be crazy. *El gran Galeoto* (1881), a wide success in Europe and America, is a triangle play, and shows that slander is often the cause rather than the result of sin. These are his best works.

(*b*) Romantic plays. Written mostly at the beginning of his dramatic period. *La esposa del vengador* (1874); *En el seno de la muerte* (1879).

(*c*) Various. *Un crítico incipiente* (1891) is a literary criticism in dramatic form; *El hijo de don Juan* (1892) treats hereditary disease.

*(1842?–1920)*

5. Benito Pérez Galdós. Most famed as a novelist (XXV, C, 4). He wrote dramatic novels and novelistic dramas. His drama publishing began late; *Realidad* (1892) was his first, at the age of forty-nine; he had written a novela *dialogada* of the same title in 1889. He was rich in ideas, but lacked dramatic technical training. *La loca de la casa* (1893) dramatizes part of the plot of his novel *Ángel Guerra* (1891). *El abuelo* (1904), from a novel (1897) of the same title, shows family pride tempered by human affection. *Alceste* (1914) turns back to Greek Classicism. *Electra (1901) (very successful)*

*Doña Perfecta dramatized in 1896*

6. *El género chico.* Playlets of various kinds, a live and popular type, based on native tradition. *Zarzuelas* are operettas with alternate spoken and sung parts. The *Teatro de la zarzuela* was opened in 1856. Ricardo de la Vega (1839–1910) was a master of *sainetes* (see XXI, A). Carlos Arniches y Barrera (born 1866) caricatured scenes of popular Madrid life. These light dramatic sketches and farces presented many social and philosophic observations, and gave great delight in their portrayal of the lower classes.

*died 1944*

Rom-Nav., ch. 37, pp. 580–582, 647; Northup, ch. 22; Mer-Mor., pp. 481–485, 526–533, 537–539.

*Pedro Muñoz Seca (1881–1936) wrote astracanadas — silly plays full of puns, etc. — longer than "sainetes"*

En el puño de la espada (1875)

Joaquín Dicenta (1863-1917) the "Blasco
Ibáñez" of the stage and creator of the
proletarian drama — In Juan José (1895)
persecution turns honest workingman
into a murderer — greatest box-office
success of late 19th century == El lobo
(1913) has convict redeemed by love
(Romantic touch)

## XXV. Novel and sketch.

A. *COSTUMBRISMO. Cuadros de costumbres*, sketches of customs, are short essays in prose or verse of customs and
types in contemporary society, often philosophic or satiric
in tone, slight in plot and characterization, and strong in
realistic description. The type began to develop in the late
18th century, flourished around 1830–1850, and was important in laying the foundation for the 19th century
regional novel. These sketches were often published in
periodicals: José Clavijo y Fajardo's *Pensador* (1762–1763
and 1767), and Sebastián de Miñano y Bedoya's *Pobrecito
holgazán* (1820). The largest collection in book form is
*Los españoles pintados por sí mismos* (1843–1844), with
articles by more than fifty authors, including many notables
of the day.

1. Ramón de Mesonero y Romanos (pen name, *El curioso
parlante*) (1803–1882). This jolly philanthropist and
common-sense antiquarian of the Madrid middle class
is the best typical *costumbrista*.

   (a) *Mis ratos perdidos* (1822). A young man from Burgos goes to Madrid, and finds much to criticize
   about city life.

   (b) *Panorama matritense* (1832–1835), *Escenas matritenses* (1836–1842), and *Tipos y caracteres* (1843–
   1862) are three series, containing most of his
   sketches, collected from periodicals (*Cartas españolas* and *Semanario pintoresco*) and various sources.
   They give vivid, sympathetic pictures of early
   19th century Madrid life: *El barbero de Madrid,
   La politicomanía, La procesión del Corpus, El romanticismo y los románticos.*

   (c) *El antiguo Madrid* (1861). A freer remodeling of his
   *Manual de Madrid* (1831), and our best guide to old
   Madrid.

2. Mariano José de Larra y Sánchez de Castro (pen name,
*Fígaro*) (1809–1837). Born in Madrid, he led a romantic
life, and committed suicide at twenty-eight. He also
figures in the Romantic novel and drama with his
version of the tragic love of the 15th century Galician
bard, Macías el Enamorado, first as a novel, *El doncel
de don Enrique el doliente* (1834), then dramatized by

Earlier influences:
  Juan de Zabaleta, _El día de_
      _fiesta por la mañana_ (1654)
  José Cadalso (1741?-1782), _Cartas_
      _marruecas_ (pub. 1793, written
                            1768)

Larra in the same year as *Macías*. Larra was a level-headed critic, a master of caustic satire, and one of the best prose writers of the century: simple, terse, keen, with bitter skepticism. He was the greatest genius of this group.

(a) *Cartas del pobrecito hablador* (1832–1833). A periodical, mild in satire, which contains some of his best articles: *Vuelva Vd. mañana*, on Spanish *abulia* (see XXVII); *El casarse pronto y mal*.

(b) Later articles. After the death of intolerant Fernando VII (in 1833) he published, under the pen name of *Fígaro*, various critical articles on drama, politics, and social problems, in various periodicals. These are more caustic in tone, and were published in collected form as *Colección de artículos* (1835–1837).

3. Serafín Estébanez Calderón (pen name, *El solitario*) (1799–1867). An Andalusian politician. He wrote *Poesías* (1831), and a historical novel, *Cristianos y moriscos* (1838), but is known chiefly for his *Escenas andaluzas* (1847), which first appeared in the periodical *Cartas españolas* (1831–1832). They are flowers of local color, with archaic, *españolista* rhetoric, and constitute his best contribution to *costumbrismo*.

Rom-Nav., pp. 502–508; Northup, ch. 19; Mer-Mor., pp. 488–492; C. M. Montgomery *Early costumbrista writers in Spain, 1750–1830* (1931).

B. HISTORICAL. The novel of Spanish Romanticism. It flourished chiefly in the 1830's–1850's. The influence of Walter Scott (1771–1832) is notable. Several writers, famous in other types, also wrote historical novels: Larra's *Doncel de don Enrique el doliente* (1834), Espronceda's *Sancho Saldaña* (1834), Martínez de la Rosa's *Doña Isabel de Solís* (1837–1846).

1. Ramón López Soler (1806–1836). The first writer of this type. *Los bandos de Castilla, o el caballero del Cisne* (1830) was a Scott imitation.

2. Enrique Gil y Carrasco (1815–1846). The best writer of this type. *El señor de Bembibre* (1844) has excellent landscape descriptions.

3. Manuel Fernández y González (1821–1888). The most prolific writer of this type.

*(a)* Los siete infantes de Lara (1853). See II, A, 1, *e.*
*(b)* Bernardo del Carpio (1858). See II, A, 1, *c.*
*(c)* El príncipe de los ingenios Miguel de Cervantes Saavedra (1876). See XV, C.;

Rom-Nav., pp. 500–502; Northup, pp. 362–364; Mer-Mor., pp. 486–487.

C. REGIONAL. Flowered in the late 19th century, and well exemplifies that inherent Spanish characteristic of regionalism (see Introduction). This type shows traits of Realism, Naturalism, and humor, and is a purely Spanish form. The *artículo de costumbre* was its immediate literary predecessor. Fernán Caballero and Juan Valera portray Andalusia; Alarcón, Granada; Galdós, Madrid and Spain in general; Pardo Bazán, Galicia; Pereda, Asturias; Palacio Valdés, Asturias, Andalusia, and Valencia; Blasco Ibáñez, Valencia. The two best types of Spanish novel are the picaresque (XV, B) and the regional.

1. Cecilia Böhl de Faber y Larrea (pen name, Fernán Caballero) (1796–1877). Born of a German father and a Spanish mother, she was educated in Spanish, German, and French. She inherited a German interest in the new science of folklore: *Cuentos y poesías populares andaluces* (1859) and *Cuentos, oraciones, adivinas, y refranes populares e infantiles* (1877). Her first novel, *La gaviota* (sea gull), was written first in French; then she translated it into Spanish, and it appeared in *El heraldo* (1849). It is a romantic story of a peasant opera singer, her tragic loves for a doctor, bullfighter, and barber. *Clemencia* (1852), *La familia de Alvareda* (1856), and many others followed.

2. Juan Valera y Alcalá Galiano (1824–1905). An aristocratic Andalusian diplomat (Spanish minister in Washington and elsewhere), a cosmopolitan, urbane linguist, cheerful, kind, witty, a keen observer of human nature, widely read and experienced. His plots are simple, and his style pleasant, easy, and classic. He is a moralist and philosopher, and a refined critic.

*(a)* Pepita Jiménez (1874). This, his first novel, has

*[Handwritten marginalia, left margin next to item 3: "wrote about 300 novels in over 500 vols. Hacker disk most of work Blasco Ibáñez worked for 7 yb."]*

*[Handwritten marginalia next to (c): "El particular de Madrigal"]*

*[Handwritten marginalia next to item 1: "in Switzerland"]*

*[Handwritten marginalia, lower left margin: "She says the frame is more important than the novel."]*

Antonio de Trueba (1819?-1889) wrote ~~████~~ cuentos about the Basque region

almost no action, but is a keen, delicate, psychological study of the mental and emotional processes of
a youth who is gradually won away from priesthood
by a merry widow, and is suggestive of sentimental
struggles. This is his best work.

(b) *Doña Luz* (1879). Presents the problem of *Pepita
Jiménez* with the opposite solution: Platonic love
of a girl for an old priest.

(c) *Las ilusiones del doctor Faustino* (1875). Shows a
Faust with no magic powers nor the Devil to help
him.

(d) *Juanita la Larga* (1895). An old man falls in love
with a young girl.

3. Pedro Antonio de Alarcón y Ariza (1833–1891). This
politician, soldier, journalist, and genial narrator from
Granada excelled as a humorist and short-story writer.
He is vacillating in ideas and varying in style.

(a) *El sombrero de tres picos* (1874). Based on the folk
ballad theme, *El molinero de Arcos*. " Tit for tat,"
decided the miller when he saw the mayor's clothing
in his own house, and went to spend the night at
the mayor's house. This is Alarcón's best.

(b) *El niño de la bola* (1880). A thesis novel, showing the
utility of religious sentiment.

(c) *El capitán Veneno* (1881). An avowed woman hater
is tamed by his charming nurse.

(d) Short stories. *El carbonero alcalde* (1859).

(e) Travel narratives. *Diario de un testigo de la guerra
de África* (1859–1860); *De Madrid a Nápoles* (1861).

4. Benito Pérez Galdós (1843–1920). Born in the Canary
Islands, he went early to Madrid. He knew intimately
and portrayed well all Spain; best, the life of the middle
and lower classes of Madrid. Remarkable are his
individuality and universality. He believed the novel
should reproduce human characters, with a balance
between accuracy and beauty. He had progressive
social ideas. His work was always carefully planned,
but sometimes rather hastily executed. He averaged
more than a novel a year. He first tried the drama, but
soon found his field in his first novel, *La fontana de oro*
(1870), a historical novel of early 19th century life.

El comendador Mendoza (1877) - _indiano_ returns to Andalusia and finds his nephew in love with an unacceptable girl who turns out to be the _indiano's_ daughter.

Later he returned to the drama (XXIV, B, 5). He is the greatest novelist of the century.

(a) *Episodios nacionales.* Galdós planned a vast series of novels based on 19th century history, to be called *Episodios nacionales.* He began with *Trafalgar* (1873), on the famous naval battle of 1805; and ended with *Cánovas* (1912), on Antonio Cánovas del Castillo (1828–1897), a prominent statesman, and on events about 1874–1875, at the beginning of Alfonso XII's reign. The *Episodios* are grouped in five series, totaling about fifty novels in all. They give an artistic presentation of this period, with elaborate, sound historic documentation.

(b) *Doña Perfecta* (1876). A progressive, broad-minded city boy (expressing Galdós' own views) comes to a tragic end in conflict with narrow-minded, small-town, religious traditionalists. A fundamental, modern social problem is strikingly presented. Many consider this his best novel.

(c) *Gloria* (1876–1877). A carefully written psychological study of love between a Jew and a Catholic girl, thwarted by religious differences.

(d) *Marianela* (1878). Dramatized by the Quintero brothers (1916). It relates the tragedy of a poor and unattractive young girl who is the companion of a blind youth until he recovers his sight and marries his pretty cousin.

(e) *La familia de León Roch* (1878). Portrays a marriage wrecked by religious differences.

(f) *Fortunata y Jacinta* (1886–1887). A long (four volumes) social study of the lives of two married women.

(g) Four *Torquemada* books (1889–1895). A psychological study of miserliness, of the "horrible anatomy of avarice."

5. Countess Emilia Pardo Bazán de Quiroga (1852–1921). Wrote various travel books. *La cuestión palpitante* (1883) is a critical essay on the Naturalistic novel. Her Realistic-Naturalistic theories are applied in her novels and short stories. *Pascual López* (1879), her first novel, is a colorful, imaginative autobiography of a medical student. *La tribuna* (1882) is a study of a *cigarrera*

1887, *Misericordia*. Picaresque novel of
Madrid — story of family "venida
a menos"

*La quimera* (1905) is partly autobiographic. *Los pazos de Ulloa* (1886) and its sequel, *La madre naturaleza* (1887), are studies of degeneracy on a Galician estate, and constitute her best work.

6. José María de Pereda y Sánchez de Porrúa (1833–1905). Vividly and realistically, with a rich coloring of native idiom, he portrays types and landscapes of the *montaña* and Santander fisherfolk. The title of one of his novels, *El sabor de la tierruca* (1882), characterizes his work. He began with a series of *cuadros de costumbres: Escenas montañesas* (1864) and *Tipos y paisajes* (1871). He despises modern city life and praises the tenant farmer, living under a benevolent landlord in a happy rural community. He has an easy, natural style, and a rich vocabulary. He is the greatest of the exclusively regional novelists.

(a) *El buey suelto* (1877). His first long novel. It urges bachelors to marry.

(b) *Sotileza* (1884). His most popular novel. It portrays Santander fisherfolk.

(c) *Peñas arriba* (1893). Contains his best *costumbrista* sketches of the *montaña*.

(d) *Pedro Sánchez* (1883). Deals with Madrid and politics. Here Pereda shows he can write a good novel outside his native field.

(e) *De tal palo, tal astilla* (1879). " A chip off the old block."

*[margin handwritten: Draws nature well – one of most popular Sp. novelists in translation]*

7. Armando Palacio Valdés (1853–1938). This Asturian has considerable scope and diversity, and subtle humor. *El señorito Octavio* (1881), his first novel, *Riverita* (1886) and its sequel, *Maximina* (1887), all are of autobiographic interest.

(a) *Marta y María* (1883). Two sisters are contrasted: one is symbolic of mystic perfection, the other of domestic and worldly virtue. Some consider this his best work.

(b) *José* (1885). Like *Sotileza* (XXV, C, 6, *b*), deals with Asturian fisherfolk. These are the two best novels of this sort.

(c) *El cuarto poder* (1888). Church, State, and People have been the three big estates in society; but now there is a fourth: the Press.

*[handwritten at bottom: La aldea perdida (1903) Nostalgic sigh for scene of author's youth — has significant prologue on regional novel — this true of other novels too.]*

The greatest strictly regional author
— next to Pérez Galdós, best author
in this period —

(d) *La hermana San Sulpicio* (1889). A charming Asturian impression of Sevillian atmosphere.

(e) *La alegría del capitán Ribot* (1899). A delightful Asturian impression of Valencian atmosphere. Ribot loves his friend's wife, but remains true to his ideals.

(f) Naturalistic works. *La espuma* (1890) exposes Madrid high society. *La fe* (1892) exposes religious falsity.

8. Vicente Blasco Ibáñez (1867–1928). Began as a Socialist politician and excellent regional novelist of Valencia, and ended as a Capitalist propagandist and commercial hackworker. His work shows prolific variety and Naturalism. He has a crude, vigorous style.

(a) Valencian regional novels. *Arroz y tartana* (1894); *Flor de mayo* (1895); *Cuentos valencianos* (1896); *La barraca* (1898), his best; *Entre naranjos* (1900); *Cañas y barro* (1902).

(b) Social novels. Localized in various parts of Spain. *La catedral* (1903) is anticlerical, and describes Church life in Toledo; *El intruso* (1904) is anti-Jesuit, and takes place in Bilbao; *La bodega* (1905) is a story of anarchistic peasants in Jerez; *La horda* (1905) is a story of low life in Madrid; *Sangre y arena* (1908) is a story of bullfighting; *Los muertos mandan* (1909) is a story of life on the island of Ibiza.

(c) Vagaries of his latter years. *Los argonautas* (1914) is a story of Argentina; *Los cuatro jinetes del Apocalipsis* (1916) is a story of the World War; *Mare nostrum* (1917) is an encyclopedic description of the Mediterranean country.

Rom-Nav., chs. 39–41, pp. 651–657; Northup, ch. 21; Mer-Mor., pp. 541–558.

**XXVI. Didactic literature.** Literary scholarship was very active.

A. BIBLIOGRAPHY. Bartolomé José Gallardo's (1776–1852) *Ensayo de una biblioteca española de libros raros y curiosos* (1863–1889) is still a fundamental bibliography of Spanish literature.

B. TEXT COLLECTIONS. A vast (71 volumes), indispensable

1950, _Sónnica la cortesana_ - Novel of Catalan coast in days of Hannibal - almost borders on pornographic

text collection is the *Biblioteca de autores españoles* (begun in 1846).

C. GRAMMAR. The Venezuelan, Andrés Bello (1781–1865), gave us our best modern Spanish grammar, *Gramática de la lengua castellana destinada al uso de los americanos* (1847). This work is supplemented by that classic on syntactic usage, *Apuntaciones sobre el lenguaje bogotano* (1867–1872), by the Colombian, Rufino José Cuervo (1844–1911).

D. FOLKLORE. Great scientific activity in folklore began, especially in the 1880's, with the organization of societies and publication of periodicals: *El folklore andaluz* (1882–1883), *El folklore frexnense y bético-extremeño* (1883), *Boletín folklórico español* (1885). The great eleven-volume collection *Biblioteca de las tradiciones populares españolas* (1883–1886) was compiled under the general editorship of Antonio Machado y Álvarez (1846–1893). José María Sbarbi y Osuna (1834–1910) made notable contributions to proverb scholarship.

E. LITERARY HISTORY. José Amador de los Ríos' (1818–1878) *Historia crítica de la literatura española* (1861–1865), still the best history of old Spanish literature, extends through the reign of Fernando and Isabel.

F. MARCELINO MENÉNDEZ Y PELAYO (1856–1912). The greatest literary critic of the century. His great library is still preserved in Santander, his native city. He wrote several fundamental works: *Historia de las ideas estéticas en España* (1883–1891); *Estudios de crítica literaria* (1884–1908); edition of Lope de Vega's *Obras dramáticas* (1890–1902); *Antología de poetas líricos castellanos* (1890–1908); *Orígenes de la novela* (1905–1915).

Rom-Nav., pp. 508–509, ch. 42; Northup, ch. 23; Mer-Mor., pp. 492–497, 570–575, 577–584.

# GENERATION OF 1898

A. F. G. Bell: *Contemporary Spanish literature* (New York 1928); S. de Madariaga: *The genius of Spain and other essays on Spanish contemporary literature* (New York 1925).

**XXVII. Program of the Generation of 1898.** The loss of her last colonies (Cuba, Puerto Rico, the Philippines) in the Spanish American War (1898) roused Spain to action. Impelled by

patriotic and national feeling, a modern artistic and scientific renascence set in. Intellectual leaders recognized the evils of *caciquismo, catolicismo, analfabetismo, españolismo,* and *abulia.* Far-reaching reforms were initiated against these evils: in politics (dictatorship, republic); in religion (religious freedom, withdrawal of state support from the Catholic Church); in education (reorganization and expansion of public education, leadership of Francisco Giner de los Ríos, 1839–1915, creation of the *Centro de estudios históricos*). Provincialism was lessened through interchange of professors and students with foreign universities; and against *abulia,* or do-nothing lethargy, there has sprung up a formidable array of contemporary geniuses. Notable have been the development of *paisaje,* or landscape, and the conflicting tendencies of Gongorism (XIII, D) and simplicity in style. Notable precursors of this period are Ganivet and Costa.

A. Ángel Ganivet García (1865–1898). His *Idearium español* (1896) is a fine analysis of Spanish character. He concludes that Spain's chief fault is *abulia,* weakness of will; hence the doctrine of *la voluntad.*

B. Joaquín Costa y Martínez (1846–1911). This Aragonese self-made man was most influential as an orator. "De-africanization and Europeanization of Spain" was a keynote in his oratory. He attacked *españolismo* and urged a break with the past, "*Doble llave al sepulcro del Cid,*" and formulated new traditions.

Rom-Nav., pp. 609–611; Northup, pp. 415–421; Mer-Mor., pp. 575–576; Chapman, ch. 40.

**XXVIII. Lyric poetry.** Various original tendencies are manifest. Poets prefer to express individual impressions more than general human emotions. Rubén Darío (1867–1916), a Nicaraguan who traveled widely and wrote much, was the great pioneer influence in contemporary poetry. *Azul* (1888); *Prosas profanas* (1896); *Cantos de vida y esperanza* (1905); *Vida de Rubén Darío, escrita por él mismo* (1916; had appeared in *Caras y caretas* in 1912). His poetry shows a delicate imagination and a keen sense of rhythm.

A. Manuel (born 1874) and Antonio (1875–1939) Machado y Ruiz. Sons of the renowned Andalusian folklorist, Antonio Machado y Álvarez (see XXVI, D).

Antonio Machado better known than brother Manuel

Antonio expresses the personal reactions of a sensitive nature to life on the barren plateaus of Castilla. He seems more Castilian than Andalusian. He has a fondness for landscape, through which he interprets his moods. He is simple and sincere in expression. He writes little. *Soledades* (1903) is his first, and *Campos de Castilla* (1912) is his most characteristic work. He is the greatest genius of this group.

Manuel finds inspiration in Madrid life, and shows technical skill and propriety. *Alma* (1898–1900) is his first and probably best work. *Apolo* (1911) describes masterpieces in the Prado Museum.

B. JUAN RAMÓN JIMÉNEZ (born 1881). Famed for his melancholy elegies. He expresses intense emotion in *romance* form. His style is usually simple, but often his expression is vague and fragmentary. He is probably second only to Antonio Machado. *Almas de violeta* (1900) was his first work; others are *Arias tristes* (1903); *Elegías* (1908); *Sonetos espirituales* (1914–1915).

Rom-Nav., ch. 43; Northup, pp. 409–413, 421–427; Mer-Mor., pp. 519–525.

**XXIX. Drama.** José Yxart's *Arte escénico en España* (1894–1896) is a doctrinal work of considerable influence.

A. JACINTO BENAVENTE Y MARTÍNEZ (1866–1954). A native of Madrid, he traveled widely, had a good education, and an extensive knowledge of European drama. He is very versatile, strictly modern in his tradition, unique in manner, and has no theses nor social ideas to advocate, but displays a keen observation of human folly. He indulges in social satire; he is a skeptic and a destructive critic, but he offers no solutions. He received the Nobel prize for literature in 1922, and is Spain's foremost contemporary dramatist.

1. *Los intereses creados* (1907). Utilizes conventionalized characters of the Italian comedy for various types, and recognizes the necessary power of evil. This is his best.

2. *Señora ama* (1908). A psychological study of a barren wife's attitude toward her husband's illegitimate children, and her change when she becomes a mother. Benavente considers this his best.

3. Various plays of social satire. Deal especially with

← _Cante hondo_ (1912) Popular Sevillan
coplas

Delicate moods → _Wehmut_ - similar to
German Romanticism - ( cf. Bécquer)
used _Romance_ (ballad) verse.

Benavente - 1ˢᵗ period 1894-1901, satire
on Sp. aristocratic society [ plays in 2]

Benavente → Best of contemporary
dramatists

sequel = _La ciudad alegre y confiada_
(1915)

In rural Castile - also _La malquerida_ (1913)

Madrid's upper classes, which Benavente knew best. *Gente conocida* (1896); *Lo cursi* (1901).

4. Children's plays. Especially interesting are his dramatized fairy tales.

5. Later plays. Show allegoric and moral tendencies. *La mariposa que voló sobre el mar* (1927).

B. GREGORIO MARTÍNEZ SIERRA (1881–1947). Wrote verse (*Flores de escarcha*, 1900), short stories (*Pascua florida*, 1901), and novels (*Tú eres la paz*, 1906), especially in his youth. He turned definitely to drama by 1910. The feminine touch to his dramas is due to the unsigned collaboration of his wife, María de la O Lejárraga (born 1880). His works, delicate and polished in style, with light plots, show *españolismo*, but enjoy popularity abroad.

1. *Canción de cuna* (1911). Pictures suppressed mother love of nuns, lavished on an orphan girl left at their convent. This is his most popular drama.

2. Various dramas. *La sombra del padre* (1909); *Lirio entre espinas* (1911); *Don Juan de España* (1921).

C. SERAFÍN (1871–1938) and JOAQUÍN (1873–1944) ÁLVAREZ QUINTERO. Brothers and inseparable collaborators. The *sal* and sunshine of their native Andalusia pervade their numerous plays (approximately 200). They are modern continuators of the *género chico* (XXIV, B, 6). They began with *sainetes* and *juguetes cómicos*, then broadened into full comedy. Their plays are rich in untranslatable local color and language. *Los galeotos* (1900); *El patio* (1900); *El genio alegre* (1906); *Las de Caín* (1908).

D. EDUARDO MARQUINA (born 1879). Prominent as a poet: *Odas* (1900) and *Églogas* (1902), inspired chiefly by love; later, *Canciones del momento* (1910) and *Tierras de España* (1914), on social and political themes. He excels in the *teatro poético*, reviving epico-historic themes, with much lyric expression. He began his dramatic career with *Las hijas del Cid* (1908; see II, A, 1, *g*). His best is *En Flandes se ha puesto el sol* (1910). *El gran capitán* (1916) depicts Gonzalo Fernández de Córdova (1453–1515) and the court of Fernando and Isabel. Marquina the lyric poet is even more evident in his sentimental prose comedy, *Cuando florezcan los rosales* (1913).

E. MANUEL LINARES RIVAS Y ASTRAY (1866–1938).

1905. _Los malhechores del bien_

_Primavera en otoño_ (1911) husband and
wife reconciled after long separation

_Pepita Reyes_ (1903). Girl supporting her
family, gets chance to go on stage – becomes
successful but loses her fiancé.

_Flores de Aragón_ (1915)
*_Don Luis Mejía_ (1925) Don Juan story
_Teresa de Jesús_ (1932)

* Collaboration with Cuban, Hernández Catá

This Galician is the modern thesis playwright and sophisticated wit. He advocates "Europeanization." Like Benavente, he satirizes social and human weaknesses. *El abolengo* (1904) attacks foolish family pride; *La garra* (1914) recommends divorce. *Set in gloomy medieval city (= Santiago de Compostela?)*

Rom-Nav., ch. 44; Northup, pp. 427–433; Mer-Mor., pp. 533–540.

## XXX. Novel.

A. Pío BAROJA Y NESSI (born 1872). From San Sebastián, he abandoned medicine to enter the bakery business in Madrid. He is interested in the lower classes and radicals. He is the modern picaresque novelist. He believes in chance motivation, as in nature. He is abrupt, hurried, simple, and sober in style, with directness and sincerity. His novels are grouped into nine series, of which we mention the four most notable.

1. *Tierra vasca* (Basque regional novels): *La casa de Aizgorri* (1900); *El mayorazgo de Labraz* (1903); *Zalacaín el aventurero* (1909).
2. *La vida fantástica* (psychological novels): *Camino de perfección* (1902); *Aventuras, inventos y mixtificaciones de Silvestre Paradox* (1901); *Paradox, Rey* (1906).
3. *La lucha por la vida* (portrayal of lower classes): *La busca* (1904); *Mala hierba* (1904); *Aurora roja* (1904).
4. *Memorias de un hombre de acción* (based on 19th century history): *La ruta del aventurero* (1916); *La nave de los locos* (1925); etc.

B. RAMÓN MARÍA DEL VALLE-INCLÁN (1869–1936). This *aristocratic polished writer* Galician was a unique and exotic figure. He is an erotic, sensational, inventive, rhythmic stimulator of varying moods, and the best modern prose stylist.

1. *Sonatas de otoño* (1902), *de estío* (1903), *de primavera* *Story of Marqués de Bradomín:* (1904), *de invierno* (1905). Portray love in life's four seasons. These constitute his best work.
2. *La guerra carlista*. A series of three historical novels: *foe, católico y sentimental* Los cruzados de la causa* (1908); *El resplandor de la hoguera* (1909); *Gerifaltes de antaño* (1909). The Carlist wars occurred through the 1830's–1870's.

The thesis playwright of the contemporary generation.

C. RICARDO LEÓN Y ROMÁN (born 1877). A native of
Málaga, he is Classic, *castizo*, and conventional. His work
is strongly rooted in the old traditions of Spanish literature.

1. *Casta de hidalgos* (1908). Creates an atmosphere of
archaism.

2. *El amor de los amores* (1910). Portrays the Mystic
triumph of Divine love over worldly love.

D. RAMÓN PÉREZ DE AYALA (born 1880). This Asturian
writes excellent characterizations, is an active journalist,
and fond of bullfights.

1. *A. M. D. G.* [= *Ad majorem Dei gloriam*, the Jesuit
motto] (1910). Bitterly attacks the Jesuit school in
which the author received his early education.

2. *La pata de la raposa* (1912). Portrays a pathologic case
of *abulia* (see XXVII and XXVII, A).

3. *Novelas poemáticas: Prometeo, Luz del domingo, La
caída de los Limones* (1916). Three cases of bitter
reality.

4.

Rom-Nav., pp. 650–651, 657–669; Northup, pp. 433–458;
Mer-Mor., pp. 558–569.

**XXXI. Didactic literature.** Scientific writing flourishes, particularly literary essays and criticism. José Ortega y Gasset
(born 1883) founded the *Revista de occidente* (1923), which is
one of the finest literary periodicals today. Julio Cejador y
Frauca (1864–1927) wrote the most extensive (14 volumes)
recent general history of Spanish literature, *Historia de la
lengua y literatura castellana* (1915–1922). Emilio Cotarelo y
Mori (1857–1936), long secretary of the Spanish Academy,
contributed much to the study of Spanish drama. In folklore,
Francisco Rodríguez Marín (born 1855) is notable for his work
in folk song and proverb. Ramón Menéndez Pidal (born 1869)
heads a large group of eminent scholars in language and literature at the *Centro de estudios históricos* of the *Junta para amplia-
ción de estudios e investigaciones científicas*, created by royal
decree in 1907, to promote intellectual communication with
foreign countries, and to develop educational agencies in Spain.

A. JOSÉ MARTÍNEZ RUIZ (pen name, Azorín) (born 1873).
Is the leading contemporary critic.

Ramón J. Sender (1901-    ) Brought up in
Zaragoza & Madrid. Involved in revolutionary activities. Iman (193 ) describe
military service in Morocco. Imprisoned
by Primo de Rivera.

   Siete domingos rojos (1927) about radi-
                   cal activities in Madrid

   Contraataque (1938) written while
     fighting on loyalist side in Civil War

   El lugar del hombre (México, 1934)
     about town's reaction to appearance
     of a man who was believed dead.
  " Sender tiene visión poética combinada
con un sentido agudo de la realidad y
conocimiento de la humanidad que
no ha sido adquirido en libros. Su
estilo es directo y animado." (Adams, España,
                           p. 315)

Ramón Gómez de la Serna "Ramón"
(189 -    ) has produced abundant prose
full of capricious metaphors; sometimes
grotesque, exaggerated, but it is imaginative and stimulating in :

     El torero caracho

     Seis novelas falsas

Known for his personal eccentricities.

1. Plotless novels, recording the author's own thoughts
   and impressions, with beautiful descriptions. *La
   voluntad* (1902); *Antonio Azorín* (1903); *Las confesiones
   de un pequeño filósofo* (1904).
2. Recollections from Spain's past. *El alma castellana,
   1600–1800* (1900); *Castilla* (1912).
3. Imaginative revival of heroes from Spanish literature.
   *La ruta de don Quijote* (1905); *El licenciado vidriera*
   (1915); see XV, C, 1 and 2, *b*.
4. Impressionistic criticism. *Los valores literarios* (1913);
   *Al margen de los clásicos* (1915).

B. MIGUEL DE UNAMUNO Y JUGO (1864–1936). Born in
   Bilbao, long a professor of Greek at Salamanca, he is the
   great modern philosopher, a paradoxical radical, and a cosmopolitan individualist.

   1. *Del sentimiento trágico de la vida en los hombres y en los
      pueblos* (1912). Portrays mankind's tragic struggle
      between faith and reason (see XXIII, C, 3). This is
      his masterpiece.
   2. *Ensayos.* Appeared in various periodicals since the
      1890's, published in collected form (1916–1918); are on
      literature, politics, religion, etc.
   3. *Vida de don Quijote y Sancho* (1905). Gives idealistic
      observations on *Don Quijote* (XV, C, 1).

   Rom-Nav., ch. 46; Northup, pp. 438–446; Mer-Mor.,
   pp. 576, 584–592.

Novels ("nivolas")

Paz en la guerra

La tía Julia

Niebla

Abel Sánchez

# CHRONOLOGICAL TABLES OF
# SPANISH LITERATURE

Iberians were the original inhabitants of Spain.

| | | |
|---|---|---|
| **Pre-Roman Period** | c. 1000 B.C. | Trade and cultural contacts with the Phœnicians and |
| | c. 600 B.C. | with the Greeks. |
| | c. 500 B.C. | Keltic and Carthaginian invasions. |
| **Romanization** | 206 B.C. | Martial, Lucan, Seneca, Quintilian, and other great Roman writers were of Spanish origin. |
| **Visigothic Rulers** | 409 A.D. | Catholicism became Spain's predominant religion. |
| **Moslem Culture** | 711 | Fall of Rodrigo, last Visigothic king. |
| | 718 | The Reconquest began under Pelayo, with the battle of Covadonga. |
| | 778 | Battle of Roncesvalles. |
| | | The last of the Moslems were not finally driven out of Spain until the fall of Granada in 1492. |
| | c. 950 | Fernán González had won independence for Castilla from León by this time. |
| **Spanish Middle Age** | c. 1030 | |
| **Modern Age** | c. 1450 | Renascence |
| | c. 1550 | Golden Age |
| | 1700 | 18th century |
| | 1800 | 19th century |
| | 1898 | Generation of 1898 |
| | Present | |

## KINGS

| | |
|---|---|
| 1035–1065 Fernando I | 1217–1252 Fernando III |
| 1065–1109 Alfonso VI | 1252–1284 Alfonso X |
| 1126–1157 Alfonso VII | 1312–1350 Alfonso XI |
| 1158–1214 Alfonso VIII | 1406–1454 Juan II |

## POETRY

### EPIC

c. 1140   *Poema de Mío Cid*
early 13th century   *Roncesvalles*
c. 1350   *Poema de Alfonso XI*
c. 1400   *Mocedades del Cid*
13th century prosifications of other epics: *Rodrigo el godo; Bernardo del Carpio; Fernán González; Siete Infantes de Lara; Cerco de Zamora*

### OTHER *JUGLARÍA* POETRY

13th century: *Disputa del alma y el cuerpo; Razón de amor, con los denuestos del agua y el vino; Elena y María; Santa María Egipciaca; Libro de los tres reyes de Oriente*

### CLERECÍA POETRY

early 13th century   Gonzalo de Berceo
13th century   *Libro de Apolonio*
13th century   *Libro de Alejandro*
13th century   *Poema de Fernán González*
1283?–1350?   Juan Ruiz, Archpriest of Hita
early 14th century   *Poema de Yuçuf* or *José*
1332–1407   Pedro López de Ayala

### *ARTE MAYOR*

early 15th century   *Danza de la Muerte*

### GALICIAN–PORTUGUESE LYRIC

12th–14th century

### EARLY CASTILIAN LYRIC

13th–14th century

## POETRY

### COURTLY LYRIC

1398–1458   López de Mendoza, Marquis of Santillana
1411–1456   Juan de Mena
1440?–1479   Jorge Manrique
late 15th century   *Coplas de Mingo Revulgo*

## DRAMA

mid 12th century   *Auto de los Reyes Magos*

## NOVELISTIC PROSE

### EXEMPLA

1251   *Calila y Dimna*
1253   *Libro de los engaños y asayamientos de las mujeres*
13th century   *Barlaam y Josaphat*
1282–1348   Juan Manuel
early 15th century   Sánchez de Vercial

### CHIVALRIC ROMANCES

early 14th century   *La gran conquista de ultramar*
c. 1300   *El caballero Cifar*
14th century   *Amadís de Gaula*

### OTHER NOVELISTIC PROSE

13th century   *Purgatorio de San Patricio*
1398–1470?   Martínez de Toledo, Archpriest of Talavera

## DIDACTIC LITERATURE

ruled 1252–1284   Alfonso X, el Sabio
1376?–1460?   Pérez de Guzmán
13th–15th century   Proverb collections

> ## KINGS
> 1474–1504 Fernando and Isabel (1504)
> 1516–1556 Carlos I (V as Emperor)

## POETRY

### ITALIANATE LYRIC
1493?–1542  Juan Boscán
1501?–1536  Garcilaso de la Vega

### TRADITIONAL LYRIC
1490?–1550  Cristóbal de Castillejo

### BALLAD
c. 1550  *Cancionero* of Antwerp and *Silva de varios romances*

## DRAMA

1468?–1529?  Juan del Encina
died 1524?  Torres Naharro
1470?–1536?  Gil Vicente
1510?–1565  Lope de Rueda

## NOVEL

### CHIVALRIC
1508  Montalvo's *Amadís de Gaula*
1547–1548  *Palmerín de Inglaterra*
1511  *Tirant lo Blanc* (transl. from Catalan of 1490)

## NOVEL

### DRAMATIC
1499  *Celestina*

### SENTIMENTAL
died c. 1450  Rodríguez de la Cámara or del Padrón
late 15th century  Diego de San Pedro
c. 1510  *Cuestión de Amor*
late 15th century  Juan de Flores

## DIDACTIC LITERATURE

### HUMANISM
1441?–1522  Antonio de Nebrija
1514–1517  *Polyglot Bible*
died 1541  Juan de Valdés
1480?–1545  Antonio de Guevara

### NATIONAL HISTORY
1412–1487?  Diego de Valera
1436?–1492  Hernando del Pulgar
1499?–1558  Florián de Ocampo

### AMERICAN HISTORY
1474–1566  Bartolomé de las Casas
1485–1547  Hernán Cortés
1507?–1559?  Núñez Cabeza de Vaca

## KINGS

| | |
|---|---|
| 1556–1598 Felipe II | 1621–1665 Felipe IV |
| 1598–1621 Felipe III | 1665–1700 Carlos II |

## POETRY

### LYRIC

1527–1591  Luis de León
1534?–1597  Fernando de Herrera

### BALLAD

1600  *Romancero general*

### ERUDITE EPIC

1568–1625?  Bernardo de Balbuena
1533–1594  Ercilla y Zúñiga
1589–1658  José de Villaviciosa

### GONGORISM

1583?–1610  Carrillo y Sotomayor
1561–1627  Góngora

## DRAMA

1543–1610  Juan de la Cueva
1562–1635  Lope de Vega
1569–1631  Guillén de Castro
1583?–1648  Gabriel Téllez (Tirso de Molina)
1581?–1639  Ruiz de Alarcón
1600–1681  Calderón
1607–1648  Rojas Zorrilla
1618–1669  Augustín Moreto

## NOVEL

### PASTORAL

1520?–1561  Jorge de Montemayor
1564  Gil Polo's *Diana enamorada*
1585  Cervantes' *Galatea*
1598  Lope de Vega's *Arcadia*

### PICARESQUE

1554  *Lazarillo de Tormes*
1547–1614?  Mateo Alemán
1605  López de Úbeda's(?) *La pícara Justina*

## NOVEL

1550–1624  Vicente Espinel
1580–1645  Quevedo
1581–1635  Salas Barbadillo
1584–1647?  Castillo Solórzano
1579–1644  Vélez de Guevara

1547–1616  CERVANTES

### MOORISH

16th century  *El Abencerraje*
1595–1604  Pérez de Hita's *Guerras civiles de Granada*

### MILESIAN

1617  Cervantes' *Persiles y Sigismunda*

## DIDACTIC LITERATURE

### MYSTICISM

1542–1591  Juan de la Cruz
1515–1582  Teresa de Jesús
1504–1588  Luis de Granada

### NATIONAL HISTORY

1536–1624  Juan de Mariana
1551?–1620  Prudencio de Sandoval
1503–1575  Hurtado de Mendoza

### AMERICAN HISTORY

1540?–1615  El Inca, Garcilaso de la Vega
1610–1686  Antonio de Solís

### PROVERB COLLECTIONS

### PHILOSOPHY

1601–1658  Baltasar Gracián

| KINGS | |
|---|---|
| 1700–1746 | Felipe V |
| 1759–1788 | Carlos III |
| 1788–1808 | Carlos IV |

*Fernando VI (1746–59)* [handwritten annotation]

## POETRY

### LYRIC

| | |
|---|---|
| 1741–1782 | Cadalso |
| 1744–1811 | Jovellanos |
| 1754–1817 | Meléndez Valdés |
| 1772–1857 | Quintana |

### FABLE

| | |
|---|---|
| 1750–1791 | Tomás de Iriarte |
| 1745–1801 | Samaniego |

## DRAMA

| | |
|---|---|
| 1731–1794 | Ramón de la Cruz |
| 1760–1828 | Leandro Fernández de Moratín |

## NOVEL

| | |
|---|---|
| 1693–1770 | Torres y Villarroel |
| 1703–1781 | Isla |

## DIDACTIC LITERATURE

| | |
|---|---|
| 1714 | Spanish Academy founded |
| 1726–1739 | First edition of the Spanish Academy's *Dictionary* |
| 1676–1764 | Feijóo |
| 1702–1754 | Luzán |

---

**KINGS**

1808–1833 Fernando VII        1833–1868 Isabel II
1874–1885 Alfonso XII

---

## POETRY

**SEVILLIAN SCHOOL**
1775–1848  Alberto Lista

**ROMANTIC**
1808–1842  Espronceda
1817–1893  Zorrilla (see drama)

**LATE 19TH CENTURY**
1836–1870  Bécquer
1817–1901  Campoamor
1832?–1903  Núñez de Arce

## DRAMA

**ROMANTIC**
1787–1862  Martínez de la Rosa
1791–1865  Ángel de Saavedra,
           Duke of Rivas
1813–1884  García Gutiérrez
1806–1880  Hartzenbusch
1817–1893  Zorrilla

**VARIOUS: MOSTLY LATE 19TH
CENTURY**
1796–1873  Bretón de los Herreros
1829–1898  Tamayo y Baus
1828–1879  Adelardo López de
           Ayala
1832–1916  Echegaray
1843–1920  Pérez Galdós (see novel)

**EL GÉNERO CHICO**

## NOVEL

*COSTUMBRISMO*
1803–1882  Mesonero y Romanos
1809–1837  Larra
1799–1867  Estébanez Calderón

**HISTORICAL**
1806–1836  López Soler
1815–1846  Gil y Carrasco
1821–1888  Fernández y González

**REGIONAL**
1796–1877  Fernán Caballero
1824–1905  Juan Valera
1833–1891  Pedro Antonio de Alar-
           cón
1843–1920  Pérez Galdós
1852–1921  Pardo Bazán
1833–1905  Pereda
1853–1938  Palacio Valdés
1867–1928  Blasco Ibáñez

## DIDACTIC LITERATURE

1847  Andrés Bello's *Gramática*
1861–1865  Amador de los Ríos'
           *Historia crítica de la
           literatura española*
1856–1912  Menéndez y Pelayo

## KINGS

| | |
|---|---|
| 1886–1931 | Alfonso XIII |
| 1931–1939 | Republic |

## POETRY

| | |
|---|---|
| 1874– | Manuel Machado |
| 1875–1939 | Antonio Machado |
| 1881– | Juan Ramón Jiménez |

## DRAMA

| | |
|---|---|
| 1866–1954 | Benavente |
| 1881–1947 | Martínez Sierra |
| 1871–1938 | Serafín Álvarez Quintero |
| 1873–1944 | Joaquín Álvarez Quintero |
| 1879– | Eduardo Marquina |
| 1866–1938 | Linares Rivas |

## NOVEL

| | |
|---|---|
| 1872– | Pío Baroja |
| 1869–1936 | Valle-Inclán |
| 1877– | Ricardo León |
| 1880– | Ramón Pérez de Ayala |

## DIDACTIC LITERATURE

| | |
|---|---|
| 1865–1898 | Ángel Ganivet |
| 1846–1911 | Joaquín Costa |
| 1873– | José Martínez Ruiz |
| 1864–1936 | Miguel de Unamuno |